SCRAP HAPPY

Joan King with Footprints Theatre Company

Scripture Union

Scripture Union, 207–209 Queensway, Bletchley, Milton Keynes, MK2 2EB, England.

© 1996 Joan King and Footprints Theatre Company

First published 1996

ISBN 1 85999 014 2

All rights reserved. Permission is given to photocopy Chooser (p 20), Facial Expressions (p 21), Running Cards (p 43), Role Plays (p 57), Piecing It Together Wordsearch (p 67), OK News, Scrap Art Info and OK Info, the Scrap Family Game and the songs from *Scrap Happy*. Other than these, no part of this publication may be reproduced, stored in a retrieval system, or transmitted, in any form or by any means, electronic, mechanical, photocopying, recording or otherwise, without the prior permission of Scripture Union.

The right of Joan King and Footprints Theatre Company to be identified as authors of this work has been asserted by them in accordance with the Copyright, Designs and Patents Act 1988.

British Library Cataloguing-in-Publication Data
A catalogue record for this book is available from the British Library.

Cover design by The Blue Pig Design Company.
Design and illustration by The Blue Pig Design Company.

Printed and bound in Great Britain by Ebenezer Baylis & Son Limited, The Trinity Press, Worcester and London.

WHAT IS SCRAP HAPPY?
- Resources to help build community
- 5 all-age sessions to strengthen relationships between people in homes, churches and communities
- An introduction to life – the good and the bad – with the Scrap Family
- An introduction to God's call to live together in peace while recognising our humanity

INSIDE SCRAP HAPPY
- Leaders' notes
- 5 OK News sheets containing the Scrap Happy Story and activities
- 5 Scrap Art Info sheets
- 5 OK Info sheets for parents and others
- 3 new songs

Scrap Happy is designed to be used with *Scrap Happy – The Video*. But groups without the video may use the OK News sheets instead.

The songs from *Scrap Happy* are available on cassette, together with songs from Footprints shows. Write to Footprints Theatre Company, St Nicholas Centre, 79 Maid Marian Way, Nottingham, NG1 6AE; tel (0115) 958 6554, fax (0115) 952 4624.

THANKS TO...
Our families and friends with whom we have learned much about living in 'scrap happy' communities, knowing that God is with us

Deborah Wheeldon who has worked tirelessly on the manuscript

Primary Colours Theatre Company, for the original stage show on which *Scrap Happy – The Video* is based

Alison Barr and Josephine Campbell for editing the manuscript

Contents

Scrap Happy – An Introduction 4

Sessions

Session 1 Signals 10

Session 2 Co-operation 22

Session 3 Reality, dreams and running away 33

Session 4 Arguments 44

Session 5 Piecing it together 58

The Scrap Family Game .... 48 & 49

OK News sheets

For groups who don't have *Scrap Happy - The Video*, to use at home and in the sessions

Scrap Art Info sheets

Creative ideas for using scrap materials and junk

OK Info

Resources for leaders and ideas for all-age groups after *Scrap Happy*

Songs

The Scrap Happy Song 92

The Scrap Cat Chorus 93

Dem Bones 94

SCRAP HAPPY
An Introduction

Discussions rage about the state of family life and what the church might say or do. Some of these debates are polarised, and many full of doom and gloom; so it was cheering to read the following recommendation in the Anglican Board of Social Responsibility Report, *Something to Celebrate*. (The words in the square brackets are our additions.)

> Much discussion in local churches focuses on what appears to be going wrong in families [and churches]. We suggest that attention also needs to be given to what helps families [and churches] work well.

We agree! *Scrap Happy* – both the video and the written resources – has been developed to assist churches in their task of helping people in their homes and church communities to 'work well'. These resources require us to engage with all ages together, recognising that God calls us to the kind of community life where love for him is expressed in love for each other. Home and community life lived in this way will speak for itself in this Decade of Evangelism.

It is our hope that, through the use of these resources, cross-generation friendships will develop and trust between people increase. Along the way, it is envisaged that participants will increase their self-awareness and sensitivity to the human need of grace and forgiveness. The experience of *Scrap Happy* should help them to continue their own 'scrap happy' journeys.

SOME ASSUMPTIONS

Every individual has intrinsic value and is unique.
All bear the image of God and therefore need family and community.
All people are human and will make mistakes.
Christians are God's children through faith in Christ.
Christians belong to the community or family of faith.
There are no age limits to this belonging.
Different generations need each other.
The community life of home and church is the primary vehicle for communicating faith.
Covert or informal learning is extremely important in attitude and value formation, and in development (ie learning through association with persons of faith).
Instruction or overt learning is necessary, but only as part of the life of the community.
Home and church life lived in love for God and each other is both an experience and demonstration of the kingdom of God on earth.
Every person brings gifts to the community.
All need to give and receive forgiveness and to exercise tolerance, patience, kindness and love.
Disagreement should be recognised and handled honestly and sensitively.

NB *These assumptions are not listed in any order of priority.*

ABOUT SCRAP HAPPY

Scrap Happy began as a musical play in 1988 when Primary Colours worked with Scripture Union to mount a national tour. A second tour was undertaken by Footprints Theatre Company, and in all over 24,000 people of all ages saw the show. From these tours we learned that adults and children were challenged at different levels through the shared experience of watching the play. Questions were raised, such as: How well are we relating, communicating and caring for each other? Is there a private face to our family life that we do not want others to see? Is Jesus a 'friend of the family' and, if he is, what difference does this make? Since then we have received many requests for further *Scrap Happy* resources, and this is what this book sets out to provide.

THE STORY

A performing theatre company, the Scrap Family, travel the country with their show – 'The Story of Luke', a modern version of the Prodigal Son which is found in Luke chapter 15. On stage the family put on a magnificent performance; but behind the scenes things are different – it is all squabbles, put-downs, intolerance, power struggles and misunderstandings. While some aspects of this family's life together may be life enhancing, the rest is hurtful, even damaging. At root they may love each other, but the signals they give and receive communicate something different.

The Scrap Family – Mr and Mrs Scrap, their son Nigel and adopted daughter Belinda – are invited to perform at the OK Scrapyard which is owned by Orlando and his sister Kitty. Orlando (O) and Kitty (K) are building a Scrapmobile in which they will tour the country – but they cannot complete it until they find a special screw which is lost amidst their scrap.

Kitty and Orlando are Christians and want to use their Scrapmobile to help people discover more about Jesus. How they will do this they do not know because they cannot agree. But they both want to see the Scrap Family's play, in the hope that they may manage to reach agreement about using it in their roadshow.

At the OK Scrapyard the relationship difficulties in the Scrap Family come to a head. Through their experiences, and with the support of Kitty and Orlando, the family members become more aware of their individual worth and their need of each other. Improved communication, greater sensitivity and more co-operation will benefit them. Running away from difficulties or pretending they are not there is not the answer; facing up to problems, learning to forgive and be forgiven is the best way forward. The Scrap Family – and indeed we all – will do well to accept that life together is a messy journey because we are human; but God promises to be with us in the adventure, helping us as we travel. Do we accept what he offers?

Orlando and Kitty are like chalk and cheese, with different personalities and ways of living out their faith. Through their experiences with the Scrap Family, they are challenged to be more accepting of each other and to pull together rather than apart. It seems that the meeting between the two families, one nuclear and the other adult siblings who are Christians, is mutually challenging and beneficial. The two families have much to offer each other, and their Scrapmobile tour promises to be an exciting new stage in both families' adventures.

WHO IS SCRAP HAPPY FOR?

These resources are primarily for use with adults and children together, and are often referred to as 'resources for all-age or intergenerational activities'. At least two generations are needed in order to benefit from them. Even for use with children's or young people's groups we advise a ratio of one adult to three children/young people.

ALL-AGE GROUPS

Here are some suggestions of the ways a church might create all-age groups:

Children's groups could invite parents and other adults to take part in *Scrap Happy*.

House groups could open membership up to the children/young people whose parent(s) belong to the group. Five sessions of *Scrap Happy* may develop into new ways of being house groups, for some of the time at least.

Parent-and-toddler groups and playgroups bring together at least two generations. See the note on page 8 about using *Scrap Happy* in these situations.

Rather than having a children's holiday club, extend your scope to include parents and others, such as older people.

Bring together different generations of adults with children in all the above situations, or invite them and the children to a special series of *Scrap Happy* sessions (eg Saturday afternoons through the autumn).

Use all-age groups and the *Scrap Happy* resources at your church holiday or for a special weekend. This could be a holiday at home or away.

Invite church households to bring the families next door to them to a special series of *Scrap Happy*.

LEARNING THROUGH SCRAP HAPPY

How do you think you learned to talk? Was it through lectures, or special lessons? No, it was through the people who loved you and communicated with you. You needed space to experiment with your voice and, as time progressed, more conversation, dialogue and discussion with others to extend your vocabulary. An environment that was conducive to learning enabled you to talk – you learned by practising speech and by imitating those close to you.

Learning to live christianly in relationship with others requires a home and community environment where we can experience and practise living honestly as fallen human beings who know God's grace and forgiveness. It needs a community and home life which takes note of the processes that occur between people and where the way is open for these processes to be influenced by both internal and external circumstances. It takes a special kind of learning, one often ignored, which is caught rather than taught: this is called covert learning.

Covert learning is caught through the climate and process of the event rather than through what is taught. It takes note of people's experiences of the process and requires leaders to be sensitive to these. The following is an example of what might happen in a covert learning situation:

> The church family outing was to the Fells. Everyone was asked to wear stout walking shoes and bring a picnic. Tom, who uses walking sticks, and Veronica, who uses a wheelchair, felt excluded and did not go. If this type of event continues in the church, Tom and Veronica will continue to receive signals of exclusion, and they will probably learn that they are not wanted. Actually, the church wants everyone to feel they belong, but those doing the communicating had not been sensitive to those with walking difficulties. How they communicated mattered. Some minor adjustments might have helped. For instance, if they had suggested walks with varying degrees of difficulty and a place near a beauty spot for paddling, games and sitting where all could stay or meet, no one would have been excluded and the whole church could have been together for some of the day. Everyone would experience that vital sense of belonging which is necessary in family and church life.

If community life in home and church is to be nurtured and cherished, we must all be sensitised to what occurs between and among us. We should be more vigilant in planning our activities, recognising the likely experiences that people will have and enabling them to learn from the process through reflection. There is a saying, 'The medium is the message'. This is true, but further thought about the medium beforehand means that more of the message is likely to be learned. This is why *Scrap Happy*, which relies heavily on covert learning, also includes a 'Sweeping Up' time in each session. 'Sweeping up' gives time and space for people to think about the games and activities they have just experienced, so that they can make the necessary connections between these and their lives.

We have chosen to emphasise covert learning because *Scrap Happy* is basically about family relationships – relationships between kinfolk, between those related through faith in Christ, and between people and God. We all learn to relate by relating. Skills for enhancing relationships – such as communication and co-operation skills – are improved by practising them and becoming more sensitive to the use of them as we relate.

Rather than teaching people about relating christianly, through *Scrap Happy* we aim to provide leaders with enough carefully sequenced resources so as to enable a process of learning that will enrich people's lives together at home and in church.

It is better to attempt something and stand in need of forgiveness, than to do nothing at all. (Karl Barth)

SCRAP HAPPY SESSIONS

Each session takes a major theme which, when put together, form an acronym 'SCRAP'.

Signals
Communication is the basis of all interaction between people, and between people and God. Session 1 aims to help us communicate across the generations, and is undergirded by Galatians 5:22–25.

Co-operation
This requires hard work. Session 2 gives an opportunity to practice playing and working together across the generations, and to discover and affirm the divine image in each of us.

Running away
Sometimes it is easier to run away than to face reality. Session 3 explores hopes, fears, dreams and reality, and enables relationships to deepen across the generations.

Arguments
Let's be honest. We are human. Session 4 gives an opportunity to be open about feelings, and to explore how difference may be handled in a way that will increase empathy and awareness across the generations.

Piecing it together
Session 5 involves piecing together individual experiences and learning to create a community that reflects God's diversity and extravagance.

At the beginning of each session is an illustration of part of the Scrapmobile. Individually these reflect the different themes arising in the sessions, and together they demonstrate how each part is essential to make the whole vehicle work.

All the sessions in *Scrap Happy* follow a similar structure: they build on each other, culminating in Session 5 which is about enjoying the group feeling and intimacy that, it is hoped, will have developed. Session guidelines are divided into these sections:

The Paper Skip: an explanation of the theme for the leader.

Rag Bag: this section is divided into three sub-sections – **Underwear** (warm-up games and exercises), **T-shirts** (games to take you further into the session's theme) and **Trousers** (more activities to take you further)

Bottle Bank: also in three sub-sections – **Brown**, **Green** and **Clear**. These are exercises, games and role plays designed to take you progressively deeper into different aspects of the theme.

Garden Waste: this is optional, but provides a good group activity to finish the games section. Alternatively, it could be slotted between **Can Recycling Centre** and **Sweeping Up**.

Can Recycling Centre: a variety of ideas that relate to *Scrap Happy – The Video*. Many of them can be adapted for use with groups who have not seen the video, especially if you opt to use the **OK News** sheets which bring you up to date with the Scrap Family in each session.

Sweeping Up: activities for small groups (Wheely Bins) that enable people to process the experiences they have had in the session.

Jumble Sale: ideas for further craft and social activities related to the theme, if you have more time.

OK News: a daily update of *Scrap Happy – The Video* with questions and/or activities for use in the session or at home.

OK Info: extra information for adults to be used at the discretion of leaders.

Scrap Art Info: ideas for using scrap creatively.

Planning a session

Consider your location and the age range of the people who are likely to be present. Think particularly of those with physical or other disabilities. Choose and adapt your ideas so that anyone can participate and value developing relationships.

 To guide you, this symbol will appear with a number written inside it: this denotes the minimum age of participants who are most likely to benefit from the activity. There is no upper age limit.

Teenagers and adults will appreciate at their own level the activities marked with 3+ or 5+.

The minimum number of activities that should be included in each session are:

- Three activities from **Rag Bag** – one from **Underwear**, one from **T-shirts** and one from **Trousers**.
- Three activities from the **Bottle Bank** – one from **Brown**, one from **Green** and one from **Clear**.
- **OK News** from **Can Recycling Centre** (if you do not have the video). Alternatively, there are several other suggestions that can be used alongside *Scrap Happy – The Video* with **OK News** being run as a home newspaper.
- Several activities from **Sweeping Up** to round off the session.

Optional extras are found in **Garden Waste** and **Jumble Sale**, although some craft suggestions may well be slotted in alongside **Rag Bag** or **Bottle Bank** activities, especially if there are younger children (under-fives) in the group.

PEOPLE

The activities suggested require people to be in groups of various sizes. In your planning, try to be conscious of how you are using groups and what it may feel like for participants. Groups should be built in ways that feel comfortable for participants, so use your maths!

Building groups

Sometimes during a session you will need what are called **random groups**. These can be identified in ways that treat all ages equally; for example, people might be grouped according to eye colour – 'Brown in that corner, blue here, green in that corner and hazel over there'. You could also use birthday months, or hair colour.

It is sometimes easier to join a big group initially, so some **Rag Bag** activities include warming-up in large groups. From the big group, use pairs that can join to form fours and eventually eights; or go into eights, then fours and twos during the activities. Ask people to rejoin their partner when pairs are needed on subsequent occasions in the session. Ensure that people link up across the generations, making suggestions such as 'If you remember the Queen's Coronation in 1953, find someone who does not'. Other combinations of numbers are threes to join to make sixes and eventually twelves. At each stage give the groups a task.

Constant groups (Wheely Bins) are vital and give opportunity for in-depth, continuing relationships. Keep them to around eight people, with one or two leaders attached to each. In the session notes, constant groups are known as 'Wheely Bins'. Each Wheely Bin should meet in every session for at least the **Sweeping Up** part of the programme where the sharing and processing of learning takes place. To form Wheely Bins, use the two-four-eight pattern described above during other sections of the programme, so that they develop 'naturally' into Wheely Bins. Each Wheely Bin should have its own space or section of the Scrapyard, which its members can decorate with their own work and so on. The groups may need some form of identification, for example a type of scrap or a colour.

While Wheely Bin groups are necessary for the **Sweeping Up** section of each session, they will also make a good base-group in which to do the activities suggested in the **Can Recycling Centre**.

Leading an all-age group

The leader's role is to enable and facilitate rather than to teach. Remember that all-ages, or several generations, will mean a creative dynamic that is very different from a peer group. Each generation will bring something significant to the whole. As a general rule:

- Children provide vision and hope
- Teenagers question assumptions and encourage re-evaluation of attitudes, values, beliefs and ways of doing things
- Adults provide the balance between idealism and nostalgia
- The elderly encourage reflection on what God has done and is doing

(From *Being the Church Family Together*, Scripture Union Training Unit)

People of different ages and stages of development will participate and learn in different ways and at different levels.

The group leader follows the ideas laid out in the session outlines (pp 10–67), using the guidelines listed on page 6 in 'Scrap Happy Sessions'. He/she should plan with the team beforehand how the each session will flow, remembering to check how it will feel for participants of various ages.

> Leaders may find the DIY course *Being the Church Family Together* helpful for planning, preparation and leading all-age groups. The course is available from Scripture Union Training Unit, 26–30 Heathcoat Street, Nottingham, NG1 3AA.

SOME HINTS FOR LEADERS

- Allow for different physical and language abilities as well as mental ability. The wrong height chair can be unhelpful. Some may be more comfortable standing or sitting on the floor, but do not keep people sitting or standing in the same positions for long periods.
- Prepare well in advance so that you can focus on people and the process they are in rather than on the next piece of equipment you need or how the visual aid works.
- Where activities are involved, try to have one or two helpers to distribute and collect in equipment, collect rubbish or arrange chairs at appropriate points in the session. Again, keep your focus on people and process and do not spend your time organising equipment.
- Watch your language! Keep sentences short. Use straightforward language and, if telling a story, keep the sequence of events clear. Use inclusive language and illustrations that are appropriate for both single as well as married people.
- When giving instructions, it is helpful not only to speak but to have the instructions written up. Those who can read are then able to refer to them and keep others 'on course'. People who are excited do not find it easy to retain a series of instructions.
- Outline the principle of an activity and explain the task in full, doing a demonstration if appropriate. Then explain the task again, step by step, while the group does it.
- Adults and children can become involved and excited when they are together, and may need time to wind down after an activity. It also helps to give a few minutes' warning that an activity will shortly be finishing. In the context of a game you will need to give them a few minutes' recovery time.
- When you ask people to listen, you will need to follow this up with another request for attention, and yet another, until you have the silence you want. It may be helpful with a large group to have a team of people scattered around the room or church to reinforce your request.
- It may be useful to work out what is expected of young children in terms of behaviour in activities. Whatever is decided must be affirming of parents and children. For some activities it may be advisable to provide a crèche for those who wish to use it. For others it may be more appropriate to encourage children to play alongside. Whatever you decide, the under-threes must feel welcome and wanted (see below).
- Sometimes parents value helpful tips, like 'Soft-soled shoes cut down noise, especially in rooms with no carpet'.
- Suggest that the responsibility for children lies with their parents or designated adults, though everyone will try to ensure each other's safety.
- Agree and explain boundaries clearly, for example 'No one touches the sound equipment except the technician'.

INVOLVING UNDER-THREES

Is this possible? In some cases, yes. It depends on the expectations of leaders and their groups. The very presence of such young children makes a statement of inclusion and enables the development of relationships from the children's earliest days. Being there – alongside though not deeply involved in the formal activities – can be beneficial for them: they learn to be comfortable with people. However, they must be safe, so they may need to be nursed during boisterous games. Parents may want to sit at the edge of things with their child, and this is all right. A quiet corner where stories can be shared and the video watched is a good idea.

Contact with other generations is valuable for very young children who will learn through the experience of being at an event. However, do not expect any formal involvement – this is too much to ask. It may be useful to have space for babies and toddlers to be looked after for some of the time, while parents work with and alongside other siblings.

The important thing is to be sensitive to the needs of individual children and their families. To feel loved and wanted, and to experience a sense of awe and wonder when with God's people, is sufficient as they learn to share the beliefs and values of their parents and carers.

These resources can be adjusted for use in parent-and-toddler groups and playgroups. However, if you are using the resources without parents and carers present, we recommend that you put a minimum age limit of 3 on your activities.

INVOLVING THE ELDERLY

Use the experience and skills of older people. They have much to offer even though they may not think so. Many are affirmed through the building of friendships with younger people. They are still learners, facing new challenges.

Choose activities that do not rely on physical agility. Make large-print versions of the songs and, if the group is big, ensure that sound amplification is good. Physical comfort is important, so do not expect elderly people to sit on the floor.

Be sure, too, to involve them in the planning and leadership of sessions.

INVOLVING THE DISABLED

Be aware of the disabled and sensitive to people with both hidden disabilities (eg diabetes) and obvious ones (eg wheelchair users). Most games and exercises in *Scrap Happy* can be adjusted to include them. If in doubt, ask people what they are and are not happy to do – for example, many people do not like doing exercises with their eyes shut.

PARENTS AND CARERS WITH YOUNG CHILDREN

It would be possible for a team to use the video and related activities with parents or carers and children under five. Valuable shared experiences could well help to foster the relationships between older and younger people, encourage communication and enable learning at different levels. Parents or carers and children may well use the opportunity to engage in God-talk.

In each session try to use a warm-up activity or game, followed by a range of familiar activities that will allow interaction between adults and children (eg make a collage together) and then play ring games on the themes. Show *Scrap Happy – The Video* and use puppets (eg paper-bag puppets) to discuss together what you have just seen. You could all learn the Scrap Happy Song too.

PARENTS AND CARERS – ALONE BUT ALONGSIDE

It may be that parents and carers would appreciate some time out to work through any feelings or issues that have been raised through their experience of *Scrap Happy*. A pattern such as the following might work to facilitate this:

- Everyone gathers to watch *Scrap Happy – The Video*.
- Adults and children spend time separate from, but alongside, each other in their groups.
- Everyone comes together again – to sing the Scrap Happy Song and others; to share news (between adults and children) about what they have done; and to pray if appropriate.

NB *The 'separate but alongside' option is suggested to meet the special needs of parents of young children, who rarely get time with adults, at a stage when their children are happy to be alongside.*

> Parents who have been to *Scrap Happy* may, as a result, wish to further their understanding of their children and of parenting issues. If so, advice is available from the Family Ministry Consultant at Scripture Union Training Unit, 26–30 Heathcoat Street, Nottingham, NG1 3AA.

Rhymes and prayers for parents or carers and under-fives together

LUKE'S STORY

Divide the children and leaders into two groups, one to represent the father and the other to represent the son. Each group sings the verses appropriate to them to the tune of 'Here we go round the mulberry bush'.

> This is the father who loves his son
> Loves his son, loves his son.
> This is the father who loves his son,
> In the story Jesus told. (*'Father' makes 'giving' action.*)
>
> This is the son who pleases himself,
> Pleases himself, pleases himself.
> This is the son who pleases himself,
> In the story Jesus told. (*'Son' makes 'taking' action.*)
>
> (*Repeat verse one. 'Father' waves goodbye sadly.*)
>
> (*Repeat verse two. 'Son' goes without looking back.*)
>
> This is the son who is sorry now,
> Is sorry now, is sorry now.
> This is the son who is sorry now,
> In the story Jesus told. (*'Son' walks home, weary and apprehensive.*)

This is the father who loves his son,
Loves his son, loves his son.
This is the father who loves his son,
In the story Jesus told. ('Father' welcomes 'son'.)

(© Scripture Union 1985, first published in *Learning Together with Under-Fives*)

Thank you, God, for all our families.
Thank you that each of us, young and old, is important.
Thank you that our families need us and we need them.
Help us to remember that. Amen.

Thank you, Jesus, that you love us all the same
and that you want to put up with all our families.
Please help us in our families to fit together
like pieces from a jigsaw. Amen.

Father God, thank you for being
Kind, loving, forgiving.
Please help us to be sorry when we upset our families
and friends.
Please help us to forgive them when they upset us.
Amen.

For the things which we've done wrong,
things we remember long,
hurting family and those we love,
we are sorry, God.

In the following prayers, everyone joins together to say the words in italics:

Dear God,
When we squabble and hurt each other,
Thank you for loving us all the same.
When we are grumpy and get in each others' way,
Thank you for loving us all the same.
When we go our different ways and don't seem to care,
Thank you for loving us all the same.
When we say 'I want' and won't share,
Thank you for loving us all the same. Amen.

Dear God,
In our families
  please help us
    to learn to share.
In our families
  please help us
    to learn and listen.
In our families
  please help us
    to learn that you care.
In our families
  please help us
    to learn to value each other.
We need each other. *Amen.*

USING SCRAP HAPPY AS AN ALL-AGE HOLIDAY CLUB

Timetable

- **10 months before:** confirm dates, book premises, check safety and public liability requirements.
- **8 months before:** involve the whole church in raising the finance and organising a team of group leaders, special-events leaders, administrators and people to make refreshments.
- **6 months before:** plan your advertising campaign.
- **3 months before:** tell the church what your 'scrap' requirements are and ask them to begin collecting scrap materials. Your congregation might suggest all kinds of unknown sources! Organise the scrap into home-made skips or tubs, such as decorated cardboard boxes, and label them.
- **2 months before:** gather leaders together and start to plan the details of the event with them. Familiarise yourselves with the sessions and resources that you need. Now would be the time to organise a course for team members on working with all ages together, such as *Being the Church Family Together* (see p 7).
- **1 month before:** hold a team meeting to finalise details. Take this opportunity to learn the songs. Create a scrapyard environment, or at least plan its layout together.
- **1 day before:** set up the scrapyard with 'skips' to hold equipment and space for the Wheely Bin groups.
- **1 hour before:** the team meet together for last-minute preparation and prayer.

Setting

Scrap Happy is set in a scrapyard, so decorate the hall with 'giant scrap'; but do this as creatively as you can, to give a sense that scrap has value. You will need space for showing the video and from which to lead games, activities and singing. Space in the middle of the room is essential, and light, moveable tables are useful for craft and other activities.

Wheely Bins should have their own designated areas and chairs on which to sit. Try to provide chairs and tables of varying heights, and equipment for people of different sizes – scissors, thick and thin crayons, pens and paint brushes. Any equipment and scrap materials for craft activities should be organised into 'skips'.

The whole tone should be one of worth and value. Junk is valuable; people who may feel like junk are priceless.

Showing the video

If you are showing videos to a fairly large number of people, you might like to use a video projector onto a large screen or a number of monitors or television sets spread around the audience. The first way works well and modern LCD video projectors are easy to set up, but they do need effective blackout and they are expensive to hire.

If you opt for the multi-set showing, it is important to understand the difference between monitors and television to establish what connections and sockets they will need, and how much cable you will need to run round all the sets in such a way that people will not trip over them. The sets must be mounted on sturdy, safe stands high enough for everyone to see them clearly. Contact a specialist video equipment supplier in the *Yellow Pages* for information about how to set up this kind of viewing.

Session 1

SIGNALS

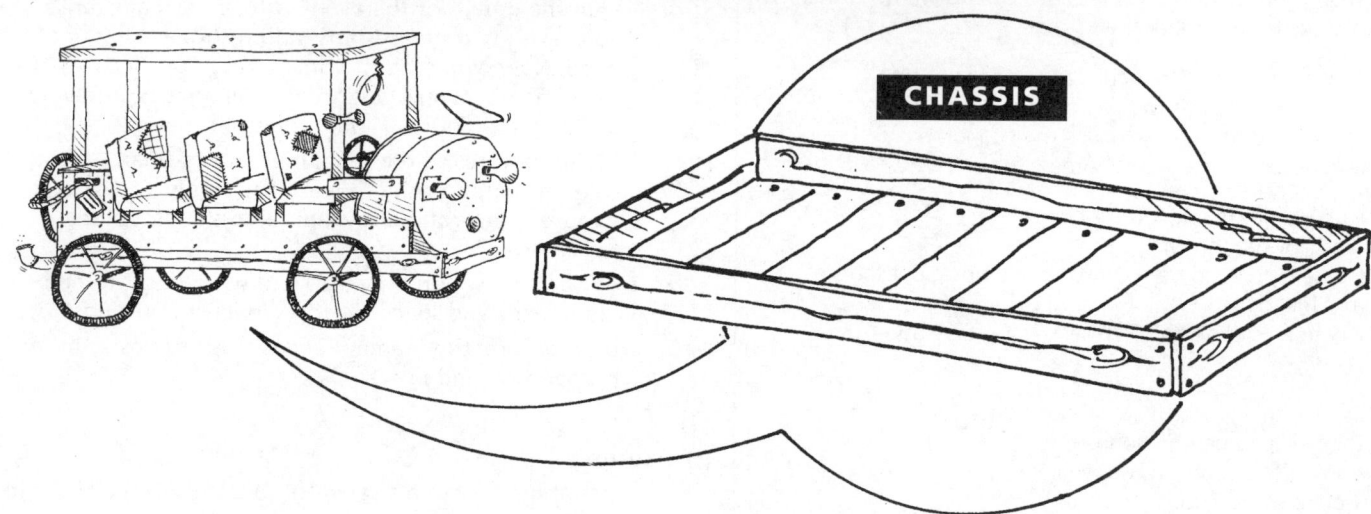

THE PAPER SKIP

What we communicate and how we communicate it is the basis of all interaction. This first session looks at the different methods we have of passing signals to one another – some intentional and some completely inadvertent. Good communication is clear and consistent where, for example, the words, the tone of voice and the facial expression are all giving the same signals. Confusion and suspicion arise when there is a lack of clarity and an inconsistency in the signals being given. Maintaining good communication is a way of ensuring that problems are dealt with promptly before they are allowed to get out of hand. Communicating positive messages offers each member of a group or family the opportunity to know his/her own value, even in the midst of a world which tries to convince us that it is our need for 'things' that gives us value.

As part of preparing for this session, why not look at the way Jesus communicated? He was straightforward and consistent, even in the difficult things and even where doing so transgressed society's rules (eg John 4:7–30). See also Galatians 5:22–25 for a list of those qualities that may influence the manner in which we convey signals as Christians.

This session contains ideas for games and activities that allow participants to play with communication strategies and discover together how signals can be passed on. As with every session, at least three activities from the **Rag Bag** should be chosen – one from *Underwear*, one from *T-Shirts* and one from *Trousers*. More activities may be used if you wish, but they should always be in this order, *Underwear, T-Shirts, Trousers*. Then choose at least three activities from the **Bottle Bank**: one *Brown*, one *Green* and one *Clear*. Again, use more if you want to, but keep to the correct order. **Garden Waste** is an optional section but provides a good group activity. **Jumble Sale** contains ideas for craft-type activities that are appropriate if there is plenty of time available.

Can Recycling Centre is full of ideas relating specifically to *Scrap Happy – The Video*, but only use these as they stand if your group has seen the video episode. Otherwise, feel free to adapt the ideas and to use **OK News 1.** They could be slotted in as a whole section towards the end of a session, or where they fit alongside the other activities. The session ends with the **Sweeping Up** section which is designed to help people learn from the experiences of the session and which therefore forms a very important part of the programme.

> For further reading on the theme of communication, see
> THERE'S NO SUCH THING AS A DRAGON
> by Jack Kent (Penguin).

THE RAG BAG

Underwear

The games in this section are designed to enable people to relax and begin the communication process by introducing each other by name.

 Badges

As people arrive, they can make the badges they will wear throughout the session. Each badge must say something about the person wearing it, but not in words. It can be as straightforward or as abstract as each individual likes. Maybe people could make badges for those they have come with whom they know quite well. There is only one rule: the message must be positive and not something unkind about themselves or someone else. Provide pieces of scrap card for this, cut into various shapes, together with safety pins and adhesive tape.

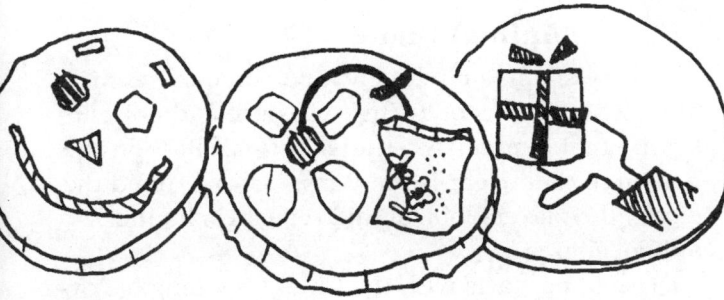

 Orlando Says

This is simply a variation of 'Simon Says'. The leader gives instructions (eg 'Put your hands on your head', 'Turn around', 'Jump up and down'). If the instruction is preceded by the words, 'Orlando says' (eg 'Orlando says whistle the National Anthem) players have to carry out this instruction. If it is not preceded by the words 'Orlando says', then it should be ignored. The players each have three 'lives'.

 Cruds and Creeps

The group is split into pairs (adult and child where possible) and the pairs line up along the middle of the room, each person facing his/her partner in mixed adult/child rows. The leader stands at the end, in the space between the lines. The line on the leader's left are called the Cruds, the line on the right are the Creeps. If the leader shouts 'Cruds!' the Cruds turn around and run to the safety of the wall while the Creeps try to catch them. A person is caught by being touched. Players do not have to chase their partners: they can chase anyone from the line who is on the run (splitting into pairs is just a mechanism to get people into two lines). If a player is caught, he/she goes over to the other side. If the leader shouts 'Creeps!' the Creeps turn and run, and are chased by the Cruds. The leader can add to the suspension by teasing the players (eg by saying 'Crrrr… Christmas was very nice this year').

 The Shoe Game

The group is divided into four teams of equal numbers. Each team stands behind a chair, one in each corner of the room with the seat of the chair facing the middle of the room. Each team numbers its members, one to however many. The leader places six shoes in the middle of the room. The object of the game is to get three shoes onto your team's chair. The leader calls out numbers at random. As a number is called, the team member whose number it is runs to grab a shoe. As soon as a new number is called, the team member with the new number starts to run whilst the previous one drops the shoe immediately and goes back to his/her team. The rules are:

* Only one shoe can be carried at any one time
* Nobody can throw a shoe
* Nobody can stop any other person from stealing shoes from their chair

As soon as a team gets three shoes onto their chair, they have won the round, and all the shoes go back into the middle. As the group gets used to the game and as rounds are won, remove shoes from the pile, one by one, so that teams are competing for only five shoes or even four.

T-shirts

 Sign Names

In the deaf community people have sign names which are simple gestures that say something about them. For this game, everyone stands in a circle and the leader asks each person to think of a gesture that says something about them – it might be a personality trait, a physical trait or a hobby. It must be something about which they feel positive. People should be allowed a few moments to think. Again, if anyone wants help, encourage that person to ask for it rather than to have others offer it. Going round the circle in turn, people show the others their sign names, at the same time speaking their real names out loud. Then going round the circle again, people sign their sign name, but this time the others copy the sign back three times – at first very small and quiet, then in the same way that they originally saw it, and lastly as huge, loud and exaggerated as possible.

Present in the Box

Everyone sits in a circle, and the leader asks the group to imagine that there is a box in the middle of the circle. He mimes the box shape to them. He then explains that the box is magic: it can hold absolutely anything anyone wants it to – something tiny, something huge, a living being, something abstract, anything. Whenever a group member (**A**) is given the box, he/she must imagine that it contains the best present in the world that he/she could ever be given. **A** then gets up and gives the box to someone else (**B**), addressing **B** by name (eg saying, 'This is a present for you, Peter'). **B** then says out loud what – according to him – the box contains. He gives the box to someone else (**C**), and the pattern is repeated.

Depending on how much time is available, the leader may want to ask the players questions. For instance, if **B** says the box contains a suit, the leader might ask, 'What colour is the suit? What fabric?' and so on. Depending on the nature of the group, he might want to encourage players to mime whatever is in the box or to mime using their present. This is time-consuming but can be an excellent group-building exercise. It could be done in two groups with two people taking the role of leader.

 Name Game

Everyone stands in a circle, and the leader starts the game by saying 'My name is… and I like…' The thing he/she likes has to start with the same letter (or sound) as his/her name (eg 'My name is Jenny and I like jam'). The next player then presents Jenny to the group – 'This is Jenny and she likes jam'. He goes on to introduce himself – 'And I'm Tony and I like tricycles'. Thus each person in turn announces the name and preference of the person immediately before, and then his/her own name and preference. If anyone has difficulties thinking of something they like, the leader should discourage others from offering unsolicited help; the person should be asked if help is needed and from whom. In this way you will avoid a situation where people are shouting out suggestions, and will maintain the prerogative of group members to ask for help if they want it.

Trousers

The games in this section emphasise gesture, non-verbal communication and the importance of observation in the communication process.

 Leader of the Band

One person leaves the room while everyone else stands in a circle. The group leader selects a player from the circle to be 'the leader of the band'. This person starts to mime playing a musical instrument, which everyone else has to copy. The leader invites the player outside the room to come back in and stand in the middle of the circle. This player has to guess who the leader of the band is. The leader of the band can change the instrument being mimed whenever and as often as he/she wishes, and everyone else must follow. The person in the middle has three guesses.

 The Animal Game

Everyone sits in a circle. Each person chooses an animal and thinks of a simple gesture and noise to signify that animal. The leader is Chief Pig and the person to their right is the Worm. Going round the circle, the players look at and repeat each other's animal sign.

The game starts with the Chief Pig doing his own 'animal' sign and then that of another animal. The person whose animal it is repeats the second sign (ie his own 'animal') and follows it with that of a third 'animal' sign. The person who is the third animal repeats this sign and does yet another. In this way, the game is passed from one 'animal' to another, across and around the circle, in no particular order. No one can pass the play back to someone who has just passed it on to them.

If a player hesitates or makes a mistake, they become the Worm and must go to the bottom of the circle (on the Chief Pig's right). The players move one space to their right to fill the empty space left by the newly appointed Worm, but the catch is that the animal remains with the chair or space rather than with the player. Thus, each time someone new becomes the Worm, a number of players have to take on a new animal.

The game should be played slowly at first until players are familiar with it. Then the leader can become more ruthless. A variation is that, instead of animals, players choose a feeling and invent a gesture and a noise to go with it. The leader must encourage people to be as specific as possible (eg not just 'sad' but 'mournful', not just 'happy' but 'excited').

Pass the Squeeze

Players stand in a circle and hold hands. The leader squeezes the right hand of the person on his/her left. Once that person feels the squeeze, he/she passes it on in the same way, until the squeeze has travelled all the way around the circle and reached the leader again. Then the game is played again but this time everyone has their eyes closed. Once people have got the hang of this, the leader complicates matters by turning a simple single squeeze into a rhythm (eg one long, one short squeeze or one short, two long squeezes). See if the group can return the squeeze to the leader in the same form as it was sent out.

 Ho!

The leader explains that this is a new martial art called 'Ho!' It has only one movement which the leader demonstrates. This involves jumping from a face-on, both-feet-together, hands-by-your-side position to a sideways, feet-apart, hands-up-at-waist-level position, all the while shouting 'Ho!' The group is allowed to practise doing this for awhile. Then they must perform the movement and sound simultaneously with everyone else in the group, taking the lead from a count of three. The group practises doing this until success has been achieved. Now they must do the same thing without the count, so everyone must watch and listen carefully to one other. This may be practised too. The final stage is when the group does the movement and sound with no count and everyone having their eyes shut. It *is* possible and engenders a great sense of achievement and atmosphere of concentration.

 Keeper of the Keys

Players form a circle and one person sits blindfolded in the middle. He/she is the Keeper of the Keys. The leader places a big bunch of keys somewhere inside the circle and silently selects someone to be the Joker. The Joker must try to remove the keys and return to his place without the Keeper hearing. The Keeper has three tries at identifying where the Joker is coming from by pointing to where he thinks the Joker is. The leader decides whether the Keeper is pointing in the right direction or not. Everyone else in the circle must stay absolutely quiet and allow the two active participants to concentrate.

 Zap, Screech, Zoom

With everyone standing in a circle, the group passes a 'Zap' clockwise around the circle, from person to person. The Zap is passed by people pointing the index fingers of both hands at the person next to them and saying, 'Zap!' The Zap cannot be passed on until it has been received – players are not to anticipate receiving it.

Once the group is used to this, add the possibility of saying, 'Screech!' This happens when a player doesn't want to be zapped; so when their neighbour zaps them, players put up both hands and say, 'Screech!' The neighbour then has to pass the Zap back the other way round the circle to the person on the other side. If the Zap is travelling in an anti-clockwise direction, it becomes a 'Zip' rather than a Zap. Each person can only have one Screech, until the leader declares a Screech Amnesty and everyone has a fresh one. When all this is working smoothly, add a 'Zoom'. This means that a player passes the Zoom across the circle by catching someone's eye and saying, 'Zoom!' The recipient can Zap it, Zip it, Zoom it or Screech it!

A variation can be added whereby each player thinks of a feeling. The leader must encourage them to be as specific as possible (eg not just 'sad' but 'mournful', not just 'happy' but 'excited'.) The game continues, but each player says the words 'Zap', 'Zip', 'Screech' or 'Zoom', demonstrating the feeling by the manner in which he/she passes it on or repels it ('Screech!').

THE BOTTLE BANK

Brown

The games in this section focus on team or co-operative communication, largely through the use of bodies rather than voices.

 Chinese Whispers

The group sits in a circle and the leader whispers a message to the person on his left. He can only whisper this once. This player then passes the message on – again only once – to the person on the left, also in a whisper. This continues until the message comes back to the leader, possibly in a completely different form from how it started out!

 Body Letters

Players make the shapes of letters of the alphabet with their bodies. The leader should first allow people time to experiment with different ways of making letters. (These must be upright rather than flat on the floor. The trickiest thing can be to make sure that they are the right way round so that they can be read from the front.) The players are then split into groups of three. Each group must make a three-letter word, ensuring that all the letters are the right way round and preferably either all in upper or all in lower case. The next stage is for the groups to create a 'telegram' of three or four words, with a smooth transition from one word to the next. The other players watch each group doing their 'telegram' in turn, and try to read them.

 ### Charades

This is a well-known game in which the leader has a list of famous books, rhymes, stories, films and television programmes. The group is split into two (or more) teams. Each team sends one person to the leader to be given a title. This person then has to communicate the title to the rest of the team without using words or sounds, only through gestures and mime. Once the first person has successfully communicated the title to the rest of the team, the next person goes to the leader, and so on. The winning team is the one that completes an entire round with each member having successfully communicated a title to the rest of the team.

 ### Picture Charades

This works in the same way as Charades but, rather than using gestures and mime, team members use drawings (no words!) to communicate the title.

 ### Chinese Mimes

This is a variation of Chinese Whispers but using mime. The group is split into two (or more) teams and everyone, except the first person in each team, leaves the room. The leader shows the players who stay behind a mime (eg changing the wheel of a car, washing up, catching a bus). It can only be shown once. The next player in each team is then called in and their team mate shows the mime he/she has just seen – again the mime is performed only once. The next player comes in, and so the game continues until the final player sees the mimes and repeats it back to the leader. The leader then shows them all the original mime. Care must be taken to ensure that nobody feels exposed. People may want to work in pairs, with some younger players being supported by older ones.

Green

The games in this section are designed to sensitise people to the importance of listening to others.

 ### Nursery Rhymes 1

The leader reads or recites some famous nursery rhymes but inserts deliberate mistakes. See some examples on p 19. The group must carry out a designated action each time they notice a mistake (eg stand up and turn round three times, sing the National Anthem).

 ### Nursery Rhymes 2

The leader divides the participants into small groups and gives each group a character in a nursery rhyme or fairy story, for example Goldilocks, Daddy Bear, Mummy Bear and Baby Bear. The leader then reads or tells the story or rhyme. Each time a character is mentioned, the leader says their name three times: 'Once upon a time there was a little girl called Goldilocks, Goldilocks, Goldilocks…' Those given the character of Goldilocks must, as a group, finish a task (eg singing the first few bars of the theme tune to *Neighbours*) before the leader says her name for the third time.

 ### Farmyard Noises

The leader gives each player a piece of paper with the name or picture of one of four farmyard animals (eg sheep, cow, pig, dog) or he whispers the names to them. The players spread out around the room and everyone closes their eyes. On a given signal players begin to make the noise of their animal. Their task is, with their eyes still firmly shut, to congregate in groups of the same animal. In the end this should result in all the sheep being together, all the cows, all the pigs and all the dogs. If there are any stray animals, it is the responsibility of the group as well as of the individual to ensure that this 'animal' finds its way to the right group. Younger children may need to join up with adults so that they work in pairs as a sheep, cow, and so on.

Clear

Observation, listening, the use of gesture, facial expression and speech are used in making a good communication. The games in this section explore these together and sensitise people to the importance of words, tone and facial expression giving the same signals.

 Instruction Giving

A simple obstacle course is set up and the group divided into pairs. Person **A** must keep his eyes shut, or wear a blindfold, whilst person **B** keeps his eyes open. **A** stands at the beginning of the obstacle course and **B** guides **A** through it just by giving instructions, like 'Left', 'Right', 'Stop', 'Go'. (Make sure **A** knows his left from his right!) Then the players swap so that **A** is guiding **B**.

To vary the game, each pair can be given time to devise their own code (ie no words are allowed, only sounds). So pairs must decide on a noise for 'Left', for 'Right', for 'Go' and for 'Stop'. **B** must guide **A**, and then vice versa, just by using those sounds. If the group is up to it, several people could be set on the course at one go, but great care must be taken as collisions must be avoided. This game could be adjusted for younger children by using a code that is common to everyone for all the instructions to go left, right, stop and go. Initially, adults or older children do the guiding! Younger children may find it easier to stand behind the blindfolded person while they give instructions. They would then be looking at the course from the same angle.

 Body Sculptures

Each person is asked to think of a feeling. The group is then split into pairs. **A** is the 'sculptor' whose job is to mould **B** into a shape that expresses this feeling. **B** must do nothing of his own volition but simply respond to what **A** does and how **A** shapes him. **A** must imagine that **B** is only a piece of clay, not a real person, although he must be careful not to hurt **B**! The activity is done in silence. The overall leader should encourage the 'sculptors' to work in great detail – facial expression as well as bodily stance. Once the 'sculptors' have finished, they stand away from their 'sculpture', and, when everyone is finished, the **B**s remain still whilst the **A**s wander around the room and look at all the 'sculptures'. Then the players swap roles, **B** becoming **A**, and the game is played again.

 In the Manner of the Word

The group is split into pairs. Each pair must devise a short, simple scene in about forty-five seconds. The scene should feature two players in a game, eg football (the goal keeper and goal scorer) or tennis (the server and the person being served to). The leader gives the pairs a few moments to devise and rehearse the scene. Then he asks for volunteers to act out their scenes. But before each pair performs their scene, the leader gives them a word without the audience hearing it. First, each person in the pair is given the same word. This word must be an adverb (eg 'slowly', 'shyly' – see the list below). The pair must act out their scene, trying to make it as clear as possible – without actually saying it – what the word is. The audience has to guess at the end of the scene what the word is. There must be no guessing or shouting out while the scene is happening. The leader should try to encourage people to be as specific in their performances as possible.

To make the game a little more complicated, each person in the pair could be given a different word. There is also a lot of fun in thinking a little about the combinations (eg 'bad-temperedly' and 'hesitantly'). Also, giving one player a more passive word and the other a more active or even aggressive word, will provide a good deal of humour. Do not necessarily match the words, eg 'calmly' with 'excitedly' and try not to use obvious combinations.

A list of possible adverbs:

slowly, shyly, excitedly, hesitantly, cheerfully, sadly, tearfully, patronisingly, romantically, violently, lovingly, religiously, famously, arrogantly, angrily, tolerantly, repeatedly, insanely, quickly, calmly, fussily, sloppily, scruffily, drunkenly, boringly, hungrily, shortsightedly, brainily, greedily, selflessly, bureaucratically, monstrously, lazily, keenly, enthusiastically, diffidently, innocently, craftily, artistically, clumsily, precisely, persuasively, sportily, richly, childishly, pathetically, strongly, incompetently

 Facial Expressions 1

Cards with very simple faces featuring facial expressions are made before the event. There are some on page 21 which can be photocopied onto thin card. If your photocopier cannot take card, they can be photocopied onto paper, pasted on card and cut out.

Players are split into pairs and one person in each pair (**A**) is given a card. The overall leader talks the pairs through the game, as follows:

1 **A** reproduces the expression on his/her own face for **B**.

2 **B** copies **A**'s expression as exactly as possible and adds a noise to go with it.
3 **A** copies the noise and expression as exactly as he/she can.
4 **B** takes up a posture to go with the expression and the noise, which **A** copies.
5 **A** moves around the room in a manner that matches the facial expression, the noise and the posture.
6 **B** copies **A** as accurately as possible.

The pairs do this a number of times, exploring different expressions. Each pair could go on to do two opposite expressions and then try mixing them, with the noises and movements (eg they might be making a happy expression with an angry noise and a nervous movement). Then the group can take some time to think about what they have just done. Is this familiar behaviour? Are there times when you feel one thing inside, but express yourself differently. Have you ever been badly hurt, but have said to others that you feel OK?

 Facial Expressions 2

As above, cards with very simple faces that feature facial expressions are made beforehand. The players are split into pairs and one person in each pair (**A**) is given a card. The leaders talks the whole group through the game as follows:

1 **A** mimes the expression for **B**.
2 **B** copies **A**'s expression but then slowly changes it, so that after a few moments it is the opposite of **A**'s (eg if **A** is pulling a sad face, **B** also starts off with a sad expression which evolves into a happy one).
3 **A** slowly changes his/her expression so that it is the same as **B**'s. If there are mirrors available, the overall leader could allow the pairs to check their expressions against their partners' in a mirror.

The activity could develop so that the pairs join up. Pair 1 hold their facial expression while pair 2 copy it and slowly change it to the opposite. Then the pairs swap round to give pair 2 a chance to make an expression while pair 1 copy and slowly change it. The activity could continue in this way so that the leader asks **B** to copy **A**'s face and put a simple phrase to it: for example, 'I'm pleased to see you' could go at first with a happy face; then **B** changes his/her expression into its opposite but says the same phrase, so that **B** is saying, 'I'm pleased to see you' while looking really unhappy. Again, is this kind of behaviour familiar to members of the group?

CAN RECYCLING CENTRE

Watch Scrap Happy – The Video Part 1.

 How Well Were You Listening?

This is a team quiz with questions based on the events of episode one of the video. Players work in teams, but the aim is to get all the answers right between the whole group and not for one team necessarily to score more points than any other.

 Mrs Scrap's Instructions

Mr Scrap seemed to ignore Mrs Scrap's instructions on how to get to the OK Scrapyard. The leader explains that he is going to be Mrs Scrap and the players are all going to be Mr Scrap. Mrs Scrap knows that Mr Scrap usually does the opposite of what she says, so she is going to tell him to do the opposite of what she really wants him to do. So, if she says 'Go' she means 'Stop'; 'Left' means 'Right', 'Quickly' means 'Slowly', and so on. Then get the players to move around the room while the leader gives opposite instructions.

 OK News 1

This section is primarily for those who are not using *Scrap Happy – The Video*, but it could also help to reinforce the video when people are at home or in a group at some other time. The Scrap Family is introduced to everyone, and opportunities arise for communicating with each other.

 Still Images

Everyone is split into small groups. To do this, Wheely Bins could be divided into sub-groups of four or five people. The leader chooses significant moments from episode one of *Scrap Happy – The Video* (eg the Scraps arriving at the yard; the introductions between Kitty and Orlando and the Scraps; the Scraps getting ready for their play) and he assigns these moments to the groups, one moment each. Alternatively, the leader can ask the groups to choose a moment for themselves. Each group then forms a 'living picture' of that moment, like a cartoon frame or a photograph, so that there is no movement and no noise, just a still, silent image. Each group is given two different coloured pieces of card and some thick felt pens. From one of the coloured pieces of card, the group cuts out a speech bubble for each character and writes on it what that character is saying. Then, from the other piece of coloured card, they cut out a different-shaped thought bubble for each character, writing on it what the character is really thinking. Is what they are thinking the same as what they are saying? The overall leader then asks the groups if there are times when they say one thing but really think something different. Note that under-sevens are likely to need a good deal of help with things like cutting out the speech bubbles.

 Button Sculptures

A large number of buttons, matches, shells or any combination of small objects are distributed to group members. They might like to work on their own or in pairs. Each person or pair uses the objects to create a pattern on the floor in which certain objects represent each of the characters in episode one of *Scrap Happy – The Video*. The objects are positioned in relation to each other as people think they should be; for example, would Belinda be close to Nigel or a long way away? Why? Where is Mr Scrap? Are the cats there?

 Scrapmobile

This is a variation on Shipwreck. The group marches round the middle of the room – which could be decorated to create a scrapyard – until the leader calls out one of the following commands:

'Front'	(The players run to one end of the room designated by the leader.)
'Back'	(The players run to the other end of the room.)
'Mrs Scrap's coming'	(All stand up straight and look innocent.)
'Feed the cats'	(All get down on their knees and call, 'Here, kitty!')
'Delivery of scrap'	(All lie flat on their stomachs, covering their heads with their hands.)
'Nigel's coming'	(All walk around the room, looking like film stars.)
'Cup of tea for Orlando'	(All spoon sugar into an imaginary mug and drink greedily.)

You may like to add your own commands.

GARDEN WASTE

 Hissing Sid

Everyone clusters in the middle of the room and closes their eyes or puts on blindfolds. The leader keeps his eyes open and controls the game. He chooses someone to be Hissing Sid, by touching that person and whispering 'Hissing Sid' to him/her so that others do not know who Hissing Sid is. Everyone turns around three times, keeping their eyes closed, and then they move around the room. Hissing Sid catches someone by placing two fingers on his/her shoulder and hissing. When players are caught, they 'die noisily', then open their eyes and move to the side of the room to watch the rest of the game in silence. The leader must tell Sid when there are only four, three, two, one people left to catch.

JUMBLE SALE

 Wax-Resist Drawings

Pictures are drawn or messages written on sheets of white paper using household wax candles. The drawings will be invisible. Colour is washed over the whole sheet of paper (use diluted water-colour paint). The wax picture or message will resist the paint and be revealed. Sometimes it is fun to swap the invisible drawings or messages so that they are revealed someone else when the colour wash is applied.

 Painting

Scrap items (eg dish-mops, pieces of sponge, old toothbrushes) are used to paint with. The backs of old posters, old rolls of wallpaper and computer print-outs provide good painting surfaces. Provide powder paints (primary colours only) and paint pictures that say something on the theme of how we interact with each other.

 Greetings Cards

People are asked to think of anyone they know who may enjoy receiving a greetings card (eg someone who is unwell, has had a baby, moved house or has a particular need; someone who should be thanked or affirmed; someone to whom an apology is due). Group members then create greetings cards for the people they have thought of, using a variety of scrap materials, such as coloured sweet-wrappers, crumpled foil and textured fabric. Other materials required are suitable adhesives (eg Copydex), coloured pens and scissors. The messages inside the cards should be kept simple: 'Thinking of you', 'Hope you will be well soon', 'Thank you'. Then the cards are posted or delivered personally.

 Telephones

In pairs – an adult with a child – use string and old yoghurt pots to create string telephones. Pierce the base of each pot in the centre. Thread the end of a length of string, approximately nine feet long, through the hole and knot it so that the knot is inside the pot. Thread the other end of the string through the base of another yoghurt pot and tie a knot so that it, too, is inside the pot and will not come through the hole. The pairs then use the telephone, each taking a yoghurt pot and standing so that the string is taut between them. **A** whispers a message into the yoghurt pot; **B** listens by placing the yoghurt pot over one ear, and then responds to **A**. Conversations can be kept going for some time.

 Playdough

The group uses different coloured playdough to model playdough people. Some colours of playdough can be mixed together to create new colours. Playdough is an ideal medium for enabling people to communicate with each other in a relaxed way. Young children and adults work alongside each other and chat quite naturally. Work on a Formica surface or on boards. A little spare flour should be put aside to make working on the surface easier. The simplest playdough recipe is as follows:

Ingredients: 1.5 kg (3 lb) flour, 500 g (1 lb) salt, about 20 fl oz (1 pint) of water containing food colouring.

To make: Mix flour and salt. Add water a little at a time to make a pleasing modelling dough. Keep dough in an airtight box.

 Music

The group listens together to a piece of mood music or some of the latest discs. What do these communicate (eg peace, harmony, questions, beauty, ugliness)? Talk about musical likes and dislikes.

SWEEPING UP

This section involves everyone helping each other to tidy up their activities. Then people go into groups of eight or so, each with a leader, and sit round in a circle.

 Music

Learn the chorus of the Scrap Happy Song (p 92) which could form a theme song for **Sweeping Up** in each session. You may like to choose songs of your own, based on the idea of good communication.

 Thinking and Communicating

People tell the others in the group how they are feeling at the end of the session. However, they have to do this non-verbally. In turn, they share what they have enjoyed the most, then something they have learned, especially about communication. It doesn't matter if more than one person says they have learned the same thing.

 Choosers

Choosers should be made up before the activity begins (see p 20). In pairs, people use them as a means of reflecting and communicating with each other. The choosers will help to steer the conversations. When both partners have had a turn, change round to form new pairs, and repeat the activity.

 Create a Psalm

God communicates through creation, through the Bible, through Jesus and his Spirit. God also listens. Human beings, who are made in God's image, are intended to be communicators – to tell, to listen and to show – but sometimes they need help to practise communicating, especially listening to one another. People work in twos or threes. Each pair/trio has three pieces of paper and a felt pen, and writes three sentences (one on each sheet of paper) on the following subjects:

1. Thank or praise God for one aspect of his communication.
2. Express a thought to God about the feelings or the things you have learned that have arisen through the *Scrap Happy* activities.
3. Ask God for any specific help you may need as a communicator. You may want to write a sentence asking for forgiveness over a failure to communicate.

The whole group listens to the sentences from all the

pairs/trios and then arranges them into an order agreed among them to create a psalm. Some sentences from different pairs/trios may flow on naturally from one another. One person reads out the whole psalm while the others listen.

 ## God in Creation

Romans 1:20 tells us that God communicates through what he has made. When we look at God's creation, we see something of his invisible qualities, his power and his divine nature.

In this activity, each person takes time to examine a selection of natural objects (eg flowers of different types, a selection of leaves, stones, and maybe a small pot) together with photographs or illustrations of mountains, seas, fish, animals, waterfalls, rivers, human beings. What do these tell us about God? After a reasonable interval, the group shares together their thoughts about God and what he has communicated to them through what he has made.

 ## OK Info 1

The leader must use these sensitively. They are aimed at households who may want to begin meeting together to nurture their home life. **OK Info** sheets should be made available for anyone who wants or needs them.

Nursery Rhymes with Deliberate Mistakes

Humpty Dumpty lay on the wall.
Humpty Dumpty fell asleep.
All the king's piglets
And all the king's dogs
Couldn't wake Humpty up again.

Little Bo Peep has lost her ponies
And does know where to find them.
Give them a fiver and they'll come home,
Carrying their tails in front of them.

Mary, Mary, quiet cheerful really,
How does your greenhouse grow?
With golden bells and mussel shells
And little boys all in a row.

Jack and Hilda went up the hill
To drink a gallon of prune juice.
Jack fell down but wasn't at all hurt
And Hilda called an ambulance.

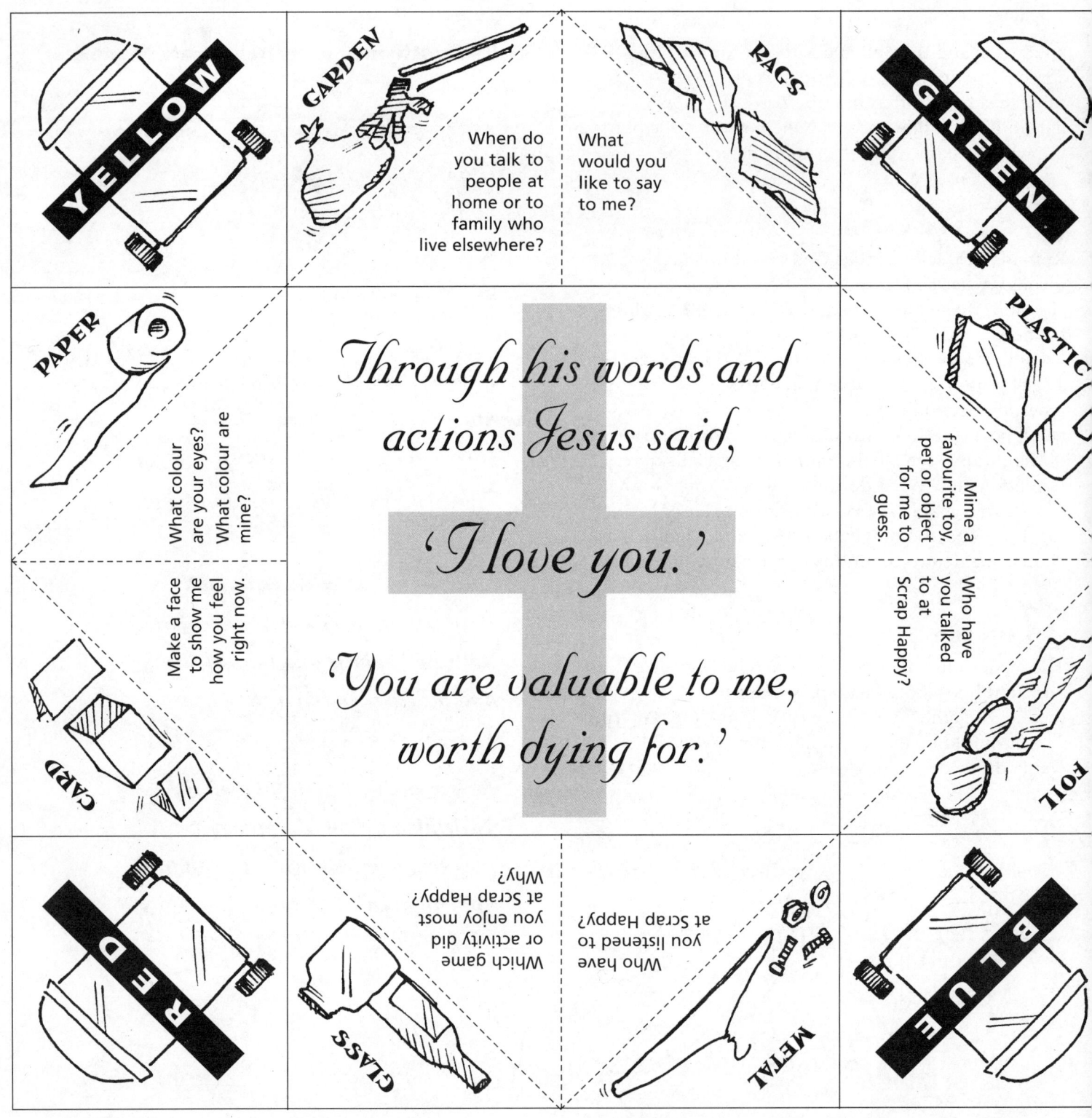

How to make

* Photocopy and cut out the 'chooser' above, one for each participant. Alternatively, you can make the choosers using pieces of plain paper, about 20 cm square. This comes neatly out of a sheet of A4 paper.
* Turn the square over, text side down. Fold each corner of the square to the centre, along the dotted lines, to make a smaller square. The wheely bins should all be pointing towards the middle.
* Turn the smaller square over and place it folded side down on a flat surface.
* Again, fold each corner to the centre, along the solid lines, to make an even smaller square. The scrap material should now be uppermost.
* Fold the small square in half horizontally and unfold it, then fold it in half vertically and unfold it, to make two creases across the centre. Then lay the chooser flat again, scrap side up.
* Turn the chooser over. There should now be four square pockets of paper with colours and wheely bins facing you. Fold the square in half horizontally, leaving the corners of the pockets pointing outwards.
* Slide the thumb and forefinger of each hand into the pockets and push them up to make a chooser. The chooser is operated by opening and shutting your thumb and forefinger, and pushing your hands together and apart.

How to use

* Ask your partner to choose a wheely bin.
* Open and shut the chooser the same number of times as there are letters in that word, eg three times for 'red', six for 'yellow'.
* Ask your partner to choose one of the scrap materials revealed by the chooser when you stop opening and shutting it.
* Move the chooser the same number of times as there are letters in the word as before, eg five times for 'glass'.
* Ask your partner to choose again from the scrap.
* Open the flap of the scrap your partner has chosen and tell him/her the task or question underneath. For example, if the word 'card' is chosen, the task is 'Make a face to show how you feel right now'.
* When your partner has completed the task, open the chooser and say the message in the middle. (NB Only do this, however, if it is appropriate for your group.)

Facial Expression Cards

happy

sad

overjoyed

angry

alert

tired

determined

frightened

hopeful

worried

surprised

fed up

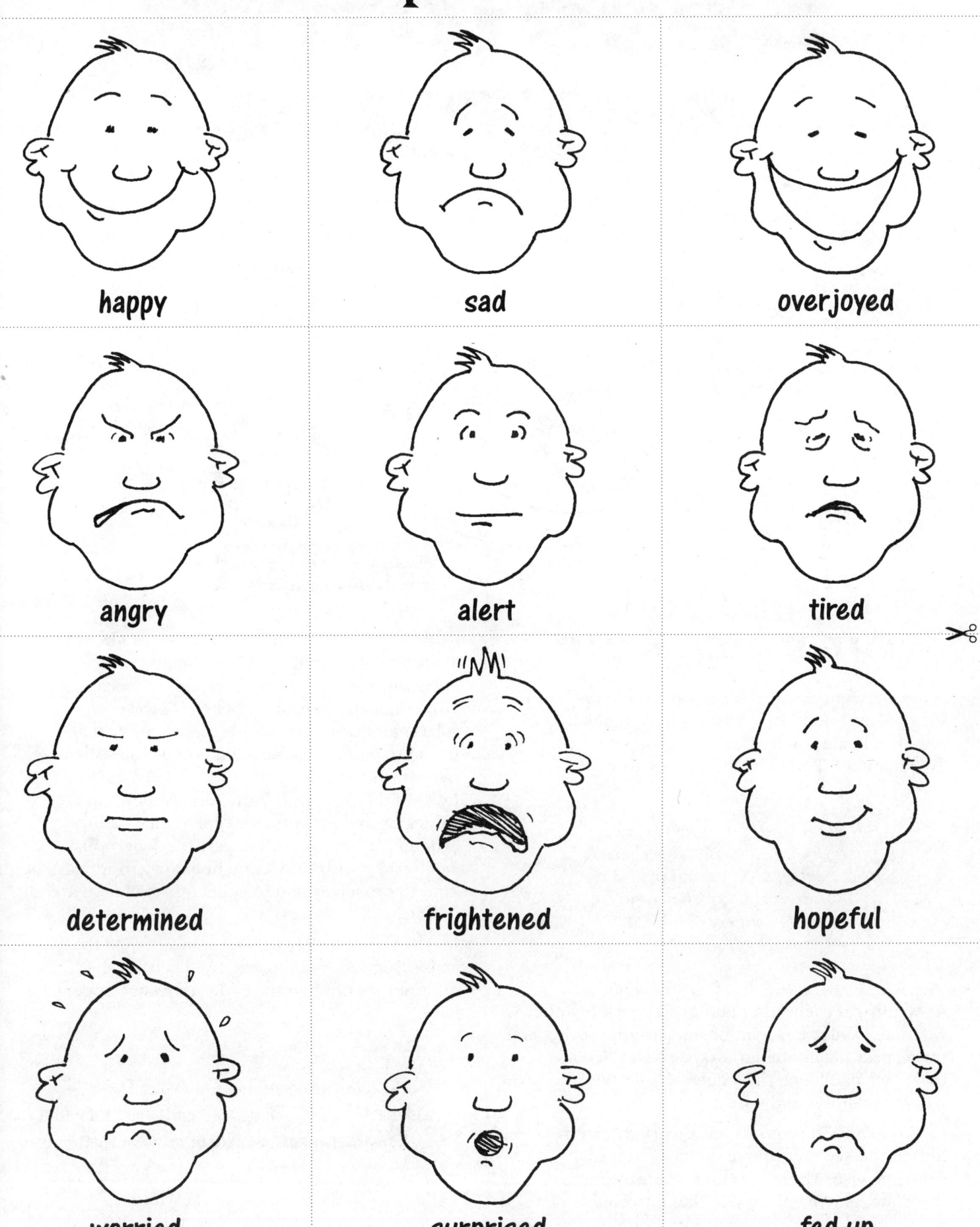

Session 2

CO-OPERATION

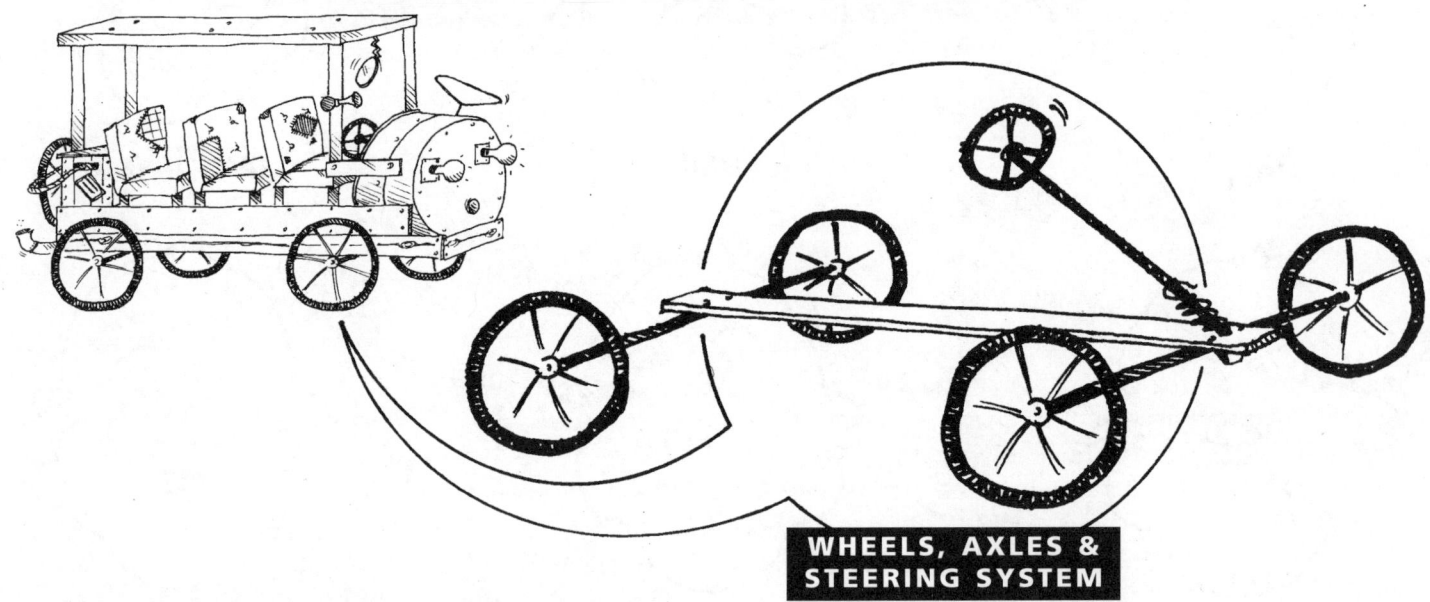

WHEELS, AXLES & STEERING SYSTEM

THE PAPER SKIP

Session 2 concentrates on co-operation: each of us is important no matter what outside appearances might indicate; each of us contributes to the expression of God's kingdom in his world.

> *If each of us uniquely reflects part of God's character – there is an aspect of God which only I can demonstrate, another which only you can show.*
> (C S Lewis)

As we affirm each other and as we work together, we model Christian relationships to the world; as we respect the contribution that we each can make, we challenge the values of a world obsessed with acquisition and with function.

Co-operation requires hard work. It can be difficult to see the unique divine aspect in someone else. There's nothing like working with someone, playing alongside them, to enable us to see their value and contribution. Equally, it can be difficult to see our own contribution: as we work with others, we may discover our own strengths and talents.

Before this session, read the verses about the 'body' in 1 Corinthians 12:12–27 that clearly exhort us to value each other and ourselves. It also states that we should each discover our role(s) and be content with them, rather than trying to emulate or simulate other roles that we may consider more glamourous. Look also at Luke 15:11–32 for an indication of how God values us and accepts our repentance – not grudgingly but joyfully, eagerly and vigorously. As we journey with him, we will get it wrong. Let's be kind to ourselves and to others, because we are all fallible.

The structure for this session remains the same as for Session 1. Choose activities from the different sections in the order that they appear here.

> See the story of THE ENORMOUS TURNIP, (Ladybird, 1994). This is a traditional story that demonstrates the value of co-operation.

THE RAG BAG

Underwear

These games will, in a very light-hearted way, allow group members to begin to work together in a variety of ways.

 Musical Hoops

Some hoops are laid on the ground, and music is played. When the music stops, the participants get inside a hoop. Gradually, the leader removes the hoops, one at a time, so that more and more people are crowding into fewer and fewer hoops.

 Stick-in-the-Mud

This is a variation of Tag. One player is 'It'. When 'It' catches someone, the person who is caught stands still with arms outstretched to the sides and feet wide apart. Caught players must remain still until a free player crawls through their legs or touches both hands, allowing them to carry on playing the game.

 Chain Tag

One player is 'It'. When he/she catches someone, the 'caught' player joins the catcher by running behind with arms around the catcher's waist. Subsequent captives join the line, each holding the waist of the player in front. The initial catcher – and indeed the whole line – must be careful to alter their pace so that the chain can function. Tactics will also emerge: the chain can trap players, although only the initial catcher can tag a free player.

 Hens and Foxes

This game is similar to Chain Tag. One player is the Fox; a second is the Hen. All other players are the Hen's Chicks and form a line behind her holding the waist of the player in front. The Fox must grab hold of the last Chick on the line; the Hen and her other Chicks must try to out-manoeuvre him. If a Chick is caught, he/she joins the Fox as part of his tail (formed – as with the Chicks – by players holding the waist of the person in front).

 Three-Legged Races

People split into pairs, and the left leg of one is tied to the right leg of the other. The activity begins with straight races among four or five pairs (depending on the available space) over a designated distance. Then things are complicated by the introduction of obstacles placed at various points of the course.

These can be either physical obstacles or tasks that a pair must complete before they can move on (or a combination of these), for example:

1. The pair recites a nursery rhyme, alternating the words between them (**A**: 'Jack' **B**: 'and' **A**: 'Jill' **B**: 'went' **A**: 'up' **B**: 'the' **A**: 'hill', etc).
2. The pair come up with the names of six flowers but no more than four per person.
3. (For older players.) The pair must make up a sentence, saying alternate words but, as for the nursery rhyme, each word has to begin with the last letter of the preceding word ('Let's stop playing games soon').

Obstacles that are tasks can be written up on large sheets of paper and placed in the path of the pairs; or the leaders can stop the race from time to time and tell them what they must do.

 Fruit Salad

Each player sits in a circle on a chair, with the leader in the middle. Going round the circle, the leader assigns to each player the name of a fruit (eg apple, orange, pear, banana). He should assign these in sequence so that, for example, apples, oranges, pears and bananas are in roughly equal numbers. Then the leader returns to the middle and becomes the caller. If the call is 'Apple!', all the apples change places – no one is allowed to return to their original seat. If the call is 'Fruit salad!', everyone has to change places. Meanwhile, the caller tries to find a seat, thus forcing someone else to stay in the middle and become the caller.

Once everyone has understood the mechanics of the game, the rules change so that the caller can say anything he likes (eg 'Anyone who wears glasses', 'Anyone who has a dog', 'Anyone who didn't eat breakfast this morning'.) The only stipulation is that the statement has to be true for the caller too, for example a person can't say, 'Anyone with a brother' unless he/she really does have a brother. Then vary the game again so that the caller has to say, 'Anyone who is good at…' and insert something that the caller thinks he is good at.

T-shirts

These games are about equality and difference. Being equal does not mean being the same. They are also about discovering uniqueness in others and valuing this.

 People Bingo

The group is split into pairs, younger participants working with someone older. The leader gives each pair a card divided into nine squares, all of which contain descriptions (see example below). Squares can be repeated and combined differently, so that each pair receives a card that is unique. Players must find people in other pairs who each fit one of the descriptions on their squares, and get them to initial the appropriate square. See how long before the whole group can complete their cards. The leader may like to stipulate that pairs cannot help each other until there are only a few people left with squares to fill.

The activity is followed by discussion about the difference it has made: people will have discovered things about their partners, and about those in other pairs, that will help them to value each person as an individual.

Someone who is over thirty	Someone who likes horses	Someone who does not have a middle name
Someone who has been on holiday in Wales	Someone who is an only child	Someone who smiles at you as you walk up to ask them a question
Someone who can drive a car	Someone who owns a pet	Someone who does not like eating cabbage

 Mix and Match

Play as many permutations of this game as possible! The game involves finding out the various ways participants can be grouped and re-grouped, and the various activities they can do once they are in their groupings. It should be quick but not competitive. The leader asks everyone to move around the available space, each person on their own. The leader is the caller. The players can be grouped in any of the following ways and any others you can think of:

1 The caller announces a number, and the players get into groups comprising that number of members. The numbers are not important so, without fuss, simply slot any extra players into groups near where they are standing. The caller announces a different number each time so that the groups vary in size from one turn to the next. Older people should be encouraged to help younger ones, and vice versa.
2 The caller announces a criteria, such as the colour of socks, the type of shoes worn, players wearing glasses or not.
3 The caller announces a physical attribute, such as hair colour, eye colour, hairstyle.
4 The caller announces the name of a television programme, singer or band and tells people to go to one end of the room if they are fans, or to the other end if they are definitely not, or to the middle if they are not sure. You thus end up with three groups.

Once the players are in groups, the leader can ask them to find:

* something they all have in common (try to make this as surprising as possible, eg not 'We all go to St Barnabas' Church')
* something unique about each group member
* a food or television programme they all like
* something they are all good at

Clearly, it is best if you stick to positives. Once the group has completed the task for all its members, they sit down. The leader might want to find out the results, depending on the number of players and time available. For example, if people have been asked to find a television programme they all like, the groups can, in turn and without rehearsal, sing a snatch of the theme music; or they can shout out the food they all like with as much volume and enthusiasm as possible.

 Unusual Facts

Each player is asked (with help from someone older if necessary) to think of an unusual fact about themselves. They write this fact on a piece of paper, and the leader collects the pieces together. He piles them up in the middle of the room and seats the group around the pile. One by one, each fact is read to the group. They must try to decide whose fact it is. Obviously, any player who knows for certain whose it is (eg if you are working with family groups or friends) should stay quiet.

 Lines

The leader asks the participants to form a line, the tall people on his left and the short people on his right, so that there is a gradation of height from the tallest person at one end to the shortest person at the other. When they have done so, he leads a discussion. How does it feel to be at either end of the line, or in the middle? The chances are that the people on either end made a bee-line for that position. How do they feel about *always* being the tallest or the shortest?

Now repeat the activity, using shoe-size, and then hair-colour (darkest at one end). If it is appropriate for the group, perhaps you could try skin colour. Discuss what is happening at every stage. What about more indefinable attributes such as holiness (most holy at one end)? Or cleverness? The group can discuss what cleverness is, bringing out the point that everyone is clever at something.

Trousers

The games in this section are about acknowledging each person's contribution to the whole – even if it is not as you would have done it, your team-mate's contribution is theirs and it is valid. The games are also about learning to be physically close to each other.

 Tossing Balloons

In groups of six to eight, people sit in a circle and toss a balloon around and across the circle. A second and then a third balloon is added. The aim is to keep all the balloons in the air.

 Patterns

Players are separated into teams of six to eight, depending on the size of the whole group. They move around the available space, and the leader calls out a shape (eg 'A triangle', 'The letter E', or 'A sailing-ship'). Each team must form the prescribed shape with their bodies. When the teams have completed the task, the game resumes.

 Touch Blue

Players stand clumped together in the middle of the room. The leader calls out an instruction (eg 'Touch something blue'), and everyone must follow his instruction. The instruction can be quite specific, such as 'Touch something blue with your elbow'. The only rule is that the thing to be touched must relate to another player (ie the player can touch someone's blue T-shirt, but not a blue chair). Players cannot 'untouch' something until they are forced to by loss of balance or an inability to reach it. This is especially difficult if the leader is very specific about the part of the body that the players should be touching things with. The game continues until everyone collapses in a muddle. Younger players could link up with older players who can help them along.

A number of team games can be adapted to emphasise their co-operative rather than competitive facets.

 Team-Touch Volleyball

If teams include younger children, a balloon rather than a conventional ball can be used. The rules are the same as those for volleyball – although they can be simplified – except that when a team gets the ball, each team-member must touch it at least once before sending it back over the net. The game could be made more difficult by stipulating that each player must touch the ball once and only once.

 Team-Touch Hockey

If the venue is appropriate, a game of indoor hockey can be set up, using plastic hockey-sticks and/or walking-sticks used upside down, with a ball made out of a pair of rolled-up socks. As with the volleyball, a goal only counts if each member of the team has touched the ball at least once. The game is made more difficult by stipulating that the teams must decide in what order they are going to touch the ball each time they want to score a goal. Or they could decide who is going to score the goal and tell the referee.

 Thank You

Players sit in a circle, and the leader chooses a player to start (**A**). **A** goes to the middle and takes up a position – any position. Once **A** is still, the next in the circle (**B**) joins him/her and takes up a position to complete the 'statue' in some way. This may involve touching **A**; it may not. **B** must not take up a position that changes **A**'s position or makes it uncomfortable. Instead, the new pose should complement **A**'s in some way. The 'statue' can be entirely abstract or make some kind of picture depicting an event. Once **B** is still, **A** says 'Thank you' and goes back to his/her place. A third player from the circle (**C**) then looks at the new shape formed by **B**, and then joins on to complete it in the same way as before. **B** says 'Thank you' and returns to the circle, leaving **C** whose 'statue' is completed by **D**, and so on. The game continues until everyone has been in the middle. It can sometimes be sustained for a considerable amount of time, with players becoming very involved.

THE BOTTLE BANK

Brown

These games are about beginning to work together in ways that could, if care is not taken, be uncomfortable or even painful. Players are encouraged to take physical care of each other – a very powerful way of learning generally to look out for each other. Players need to take responsibility for their own safety and that of others, especially the more vulnerable group members.

 Pairs

In pairs, each person partnered with someone of roughly the same size, the group plays 'see-saws': people sit with legs crossed on the floor, facing their partners and holding their hands with arms at full stretch. The pair can then rock backwards and forwards. This only works if people co-operate and care for each other. Then the pairs sit back-to-back with their arms folded – backs need to touch – and stand up by pushing against each other to help each other rise to their feet.

 Rock and Snakes

Choose one or two players to be Snakes, depending on the size of the group. The rest of the group form a firm, interlocking, imaginative structure, which is the Rock. Some people can be on hands and knees, others bending, some crouching down or leaning across others. It is important that the structure is firm, that everyone is comfortable and that they can all hold their positions for a while. The Snakes crawl over, under and through the Rock, exploring all of its niches, nooks and crannies. Encourage the Snakes to be as adventurous as they dare. (It is helpful if the Snakes remove their watches, belts with buckles, jewellery and shoes, and for players to wear comfortable tracksuits or jeans.) Stop the activity and choose one or two other people to be Snakes, giving the Rock the chance to stretch and re-form in a new way.

 Machines

The leader asks one player (**A**) to stand still except for doing a single action and making a simple noise. The noise and action must be repeated, maintaining as constant a speed and rhythm as possible, only stopping when the leader tells **A** to stop. Then the leader asks a second person (**B**) to join in and make another (different) action and noise simultaneously with **A**. **B** works at exactly the same speed and rhythm, taking his cue from **A**. Gradually, more people are added, one at a time, until the whole group is involved. Each person should know who to watch for his/her cue; each should only be watching one other player. When everyone is involved, the leader allows them to rest, and then changes the rules so that **A** will take his cue from the leader, but everyone else must focus and imitate only the person they are already following.

The leader agrees with **A** the signals for 'Go', 'Stop', 'Speed up' and 'Slow down'. He will be able to control the whole 'machine' by communicating only with **A**. When he starts the group and stops them, the effects should ripple through the 'machine' gradually rather than all at once.

 Body-Part Points

Players are grouped into teams of around six people. Each part of the body is assigned a different score (eg hands and feet = 1 point each; knees and elbows = 3 points each; back = 6 points; stomach = 5 points; shoulders = 4 points each, or 7 points for across the back of the shoulders; the top of the head = 15 points). The leader calls out a number, and each team has to achieve that number by adding up the scores of any members' body-parts that are touching the floor. In other words, with their bodies team members must together create a group 'structure' that is supported on the floor only by enough body-parts to make the appropriate score.

Clearly, the easiest numbers to start with – if players are in groups of six – are 12 and then 6. See what happens with very large numbers and with quite small numbers. What happens when the scoring is reversed so that 'easy' body-parts like hands and feet score very highly, and body-parts such as heads score very low?

 Boat Race

Players create 'boats' by forming lines of six to ten people, depending on the size of the group and the space available. Boats are created by players squatting with their knees fully bent, all facing the same way and holding the shoulders of the person in front. Each Boat has a Cox who stands facing the Boat and holding the hands of the player at the front of the boat. The Boat moves when all the players simultaneously spring off both feet and jump forward the same distance. It is the job of the Cox to call the rhythm. Teams should be given some time to experiment with different Coxes and with different configurations of players. Is it better to have small players in front or behind? Then the Boats can race each other.

Green

In this section the games create a process and a result in which each group member is an active contributor.

 Spirals

The group forms a large circle and everyone holds hands. The leader breaks the circle at one point, then goes round and round and round inside the circle, pulling the others in his wake so that they create a spiral. On reaching the middle, the leader does an about-turn and continues until the outside circle is back in place.

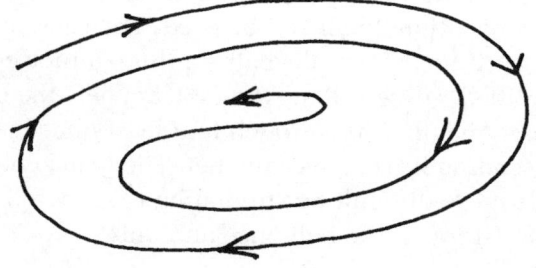

Name Animals

Each person finds a way of saying his/her name – repeating it so that it sounds like the call of a bird or the noise of an animal – and devises a way of travelling around the room that goes with their name-noise. The players then pair up with others, creating a new name-noise and a new way of travelling, which they do together and which is a fusion of all or part of their original noises and movements. These pairs join other pairs, and then fours join other fours, and so on, at each stage creating a new name-noise and corporate motion that fuses elements of the previous components. Eventually, all the players combine to create a group name-noise and method of travelling around the room. The name-noise might be quite long; the leader must encourage the group to use any mechanism (eg rhythm, melody) to make it easy to remember. Every group member needs to be an active participant.

 The Schoenberg Game

This game can take a long time, and different groups will need different levels of help and support. The players begin by working individually. Each person must find a way of completing three tasks:

1. Move from a standing position to a position sitting on the floor.
2. Create a rhythm using seven hand-claps.
3. Complete the sentence 'Everyone is important because...'.

When everyone has achieved this, they go into pairs. Each person must negotiate with their partner so that the three tasks are achieved in such a way that the pair are both doing exactly the same thing at exactly the same time and speed. When it comes to completing the sentence, they must say something together with which they both agree. Then pair up the pairs, and so on (as in Name Animals), until eventually the whole group is negotiating with each other on a physical task, a task that involves rhythm and an ideological task. They should all reach a point where they are doing and saying exactly the same thing at exactly the same time, creating a real sense of achievement. The leader can then encourage the group to reflect on the *process* of the activity not just on the end result.

Clear

The following games are about working together and looking out for each other, learning to contribute, to trust and to be trusted, so as to create something with someone else. The leader must not go beyond his own confidence level as it is important that he remains in control.

 Pairs

Pairs of similar height stand facing each other a little more than arms' length apart. Arms are held out in front so that hands push against each other when both partners are leaning forward. Partners then push hard enough for the pair to sway backwards and forwards, creating a safe rhythm. The skill is to keep each other safe by applying just the right amount of pressure to the hands. Keep this going for a couple of minutes.

 Mirrors and Shadows

Players works in pairs, **A** and **B**. The pairs sit on the floor or on chairs, facing each other and close enough so that their knees almost touch. **A** leads first: **B** is **A**'s mirror. **A** moves his/her hands and arms slowly and smoothly so that **B** can follow them exactly as if **B** were **A**'s reflection in a mirror. **A** is not trying to catch **B** out; rather the pairs are working together to create the impression of mirroring. Then the roles are swapped over so that **B** leads. Then half the group is invited to watch the other half, and vice versa. Each pair decides who will lead, and the observers must see if they can tell who the leader is.

Extend the exercise so that whoever is leading can move his/her whole body. Movements still need to be very slow and very controlled. People must also be sensitive not only to their own physical limitations of being in control but also to those of their partner.

The exercise then changes so that **B** sits behind **A** and shadows rather than mirrors what **A** does. Then they swap roles again. This part of the exercise can be varied by placing the whole group in a line around the room, all sitting down and facing the same way. The person at the front moves their arms and hands slowly and smoothly; the person behind shadows them. The third person shadows the second, the fourth shadows the third, and so on. An effective rippling momentum is set up which can be very beautiful. Move the front person to the back to give others a chance to lead.

The following Trust Exercises should all be done in complete silence, or with gentle music playing in the background. Concentration should be maintained. Pairs are encouraged to monitor themselves: if their concentration slips, the exercise should be stopped and started again when they are ready.

 Trust Exercises 1

These should be done as a group of exercises and in the sequence that appears here. The group works in pairs, **A** and **B**, and silence should be maintained until the final exercise.

1   **B** shuts his eyes and lets **A** take him by the hand and elbow and lead him slowly around the room. **A** must ensure that **B** doesn't bump into anyone or anything. (Depending on the space available, it may be that only half of the whole group can do this at any one time.)
2   Roles are swapped so that **B** leads **A**. The person who is leading must be sensitive to the level of confidence that his/her partner has, and not frighten them. These games are about building trust, not demonstrating bravado.
3   **A** leads **B** using only fingertip contact. **B**'s left index finger is placed on top of **A**'s right index finger, and the pairs move around the room. Then roles are swapped.
4   There is no physical contact at all. **A** breaks the silence only to call **B**'s name, and **B** follows the sound of **A**'s voice. **A** needs to be aware of the way he/she sounds – only calling **B**'s name but communicating danger, for example, by volume and urgency. The roles are reversed again.

The group can briefly discuss these exercises after each one. Which is easier, leading or being led? Is the exercise itself easy or hard? If the pairs are mixed up, does it make a difference? Again, if a pair loses concentration, they should be encouraged to stop, rest a moment and then start again. If any pair is disrupting the exercise for others, ask them to sit out for a while until they have regained their concentration.

The next stage of the exercise has the group standing in a circle. A volunteer walks slowly across the circle with his eyes shut. When he reaches the other side, the group member(s) on that side gently receives the volunteer, turns him around and sends him back across the circle again. After a while, ask the volunteer to open his eyes and give someone else a turn. After a couple of people have had a go, someone new can take a turn and when he/she is

established, allow that person to keep going while someone else is sent across the circle. As many people can be sent across the circle as the leader feels he can control.

 Trust Exercises 2

People are split into small groups of eight or into Wheely Bin groups. One player stands with his eyes shut in the middle of each group. The rest stand round in a circle, close to this player and to each other. The feet of the person in the middle remain still and firmly planted on the floor with the body straight. Keeping firm but relaxed, the player then allows the group to pass him around and across the circle. The group must try to sense how he is feeling and, if appropriate, they can move out slightly. They must also be sensitive to each other. They may need to move around as they offer support, to ensure that the middle player does not fall. The aim of this exercise is for the person in the middle to have an enjoyable experience.

After a while the leader stops the exercise, reminding those in the circles to ensure that the players in the middle are standing safely. These players then open their eyes and rejoin their group, giving others who want to have a go the opportunity to be passed around the circle.

 Human Knot

People are split into small groups of eight or ten. Each group stands in a circle and each person stretches their arms out in front of them. With each hand, a player grasps hold of the hands of two other players. Players cannot hold both hands of the same person but only one, and they cannot hold the hand of the person next to them in the circle. The task then is for the group to untangle itself into a circle (or two interlocking circles) without letting go of their hands, although a group member may change his/her grip to avoid broken wrists! If the groups get on well with this, the leader can ask them to do it without speaking, in complete silence.

 Limits

The group reflect together on 'The Story of Luke' (OK News 2), especially on Luke himself, his relationship with his father and his experiences away from home. What might Luke have learned from those experiences? To what extent was he 'finding himself'?

What of the father? In the Bible version of the story (Luke 15:11–32) he is sometimes described as 'the loving father'. How did he express his love to his son? In what ways was he a responsible parent in letting his son go off to make so many mistakes?

After the group has shared their thoughts on these questions, they listen to the poem 'Limits' by Ulrich Schaffer:

*Father, I don't know where my limits are;
where the boundaries are
in which I must live.*

*You give me a freedom
I don't want and can't handle
even if sometimes I ask for it,
because that freedom creates an
 insecurity in me
and I don't know quite how to live.*

*Please be firm and clear
and let me feel your love that way;
and realise that I must buck
against what you are saying
to find myself,
to learn that I am much more
than an extension of you.*

(From FOR THE LOVE OF CHILDREN, Lion Publishing, 1979)

Now group members take time to reflect individually on their own experiences of 'leaving' at various stages of life, and of 'bucking' against parents and others in parent roles. Parents can share together experiences of letting children go at various stages of their lives (ie from going into a crèche for the first time to leaving home to live in a flat-share, or similar).

CAN RECYCLING CENTRE

Watch Scrap Happy – The Video Part 2.

 **OK News 2**

In fours or more, group members take the parts of Luke, his father and his brother, and read 'The Story of Luke'. On large, separate sheets of paper, the groups draw each character from the play and name them. Together they talk about each character from the play in turn, discussing especially their qualities. Points about the characters can be written down on their individual sheets. Group members can write down what they would like to say to these characters about their family relationships by the end of the story. For each character, the players must find something good that they appreciate about them, and something that each character needs to say to the other two.

NB It will probably be better to engage younger members in colouring or decorating the figures while the others take part in the discussion. This way younger members can still listen and contribute while being occupied.

 Mask-Making

People can make masks to represent the different members of the Scrap Family in episode two of the Scrap Happy story. The masks can be of any type – whole head, whole face or half-face – and they can be as ambitious or as simple as people like. Masks could be made that represent the different moods of the Scrap Happy characters. Some ideas may be found on **Scrap Art Info 3**. When everyone has finished their masks, they can use them in pairs or fours to have conversations as members of the Scrap Family.

 Singing

The players learn the verses and chorus of the Scrap Happy Song, and work out actions to go with the verses.

 Rhyme

For parents and under-fives together:

Luke took his money
    (Clasp imaginary money-bag in each hand.)
And went far away
    (Make fingers 'walk'.)
To buy all the things
That he wanted one day.
    (Outline large circle with arms.)
His father was sad
    (Make sad face.)
That his dear son had gone,
    (Wave goodbye.)
But Luke spent his money
    (Mime payment and taking goods.)
And had lots of fun.
    (Make happy face.)
Soon all his money was gone.
    (Show empty hands.)
No food could be had,
    (Shake head slowly.)
So Luke looked after pigs
    (Screw up nose and grunt like pig.)
And was hungry and sad.
    (Make sad face and rub tummy.)

He went home to his father
   (Make fingers walk.)
And said, 'I am sorry.'
   (Downcast eyes.)
His father forgave him,
   (Mime hugging action.)
And they had a big party.
   (Mime eating and drinking.)

(© Scripture Union 1985, first published in
LEARNING TOGETHER WITH UNDER-FIVES)

 Perform 'The Story of Luke'

The story (OK News 2) is divided into sections, and different sections are assigned to small groups. The groups are given time to rehearse and then hold a grand performance, putting the sections together in the right order. People can use ideas from *Scrap Happy – The Video*, adding or adapting these to create their own version. This activity can be varied (if a group seems keen and up to it) by taking another Bible story, like the Good Samaritan, and giving it the same treatment, perhaps using rhythm and rhyme to create the script, along with some ingenious physical movements. Again, the small groups can work on different sections, giving an interesting, finished whole.

 Design the Scrapmobile

Drawings, plans, sketches can be made, as well as models, from any construction materials or from junk. People work in groups or individually to design the vehicle. What would be in it? Who would be on it? Why? What personal things would they take with them if they were going 'on tour' in the Scrapmobile?

 Scrap Animals

If the members of the Scrap Family and Kitty and Orlando were animals, what kind of animals would they be and why? Group members draw or paint their ideas and share them with others.

GARDEN WASTE

 Bomb Disposal

(If the group is very large, people may have to be put in different rooms, or the group split in half, with one half taking part in the activity and the other observing them.)

The leader places an alarm clock at one end of the room and explains that the group must pretend it is a bomb. One person in the group is given some string (or rope, washing line, etc) that is at least almost as long as the room. The group is sent to the end of the room away from the alarm clock. The leader asks them to imagine that the floor is actually a wall. The whole group lie down so that their feet touch the wall opposite the alarm clock, which is now designated as the floor. Their task is to 'climb up the wall' to reach the alarm clock. They can use furniture (which you may have to place strategically), each other and the string (which they are to imagine is a strong rope). They must remain true to their orientation as they climb. The alarm clock is set to go off in ten minutes. To turn it off and thus defuse the bomb, they each have to reach the clock and touch it.

JUMBLE SALE

 Puppets

For this activity the group makes puppets from scrap materials. See **Scrap Art Info 4** for ideas. Then the puppets can be used to tell stories (eg the Lost Son from Luke chapter 15). The leader can encourage participants to use their puppets and talk about the characters the puppets are playing.

 Eggshell Mosaics

Beautiful mosaics can be created from eggshells that have been painted in bright colours and then broken. Work in cross-generational groups of three or four people, so that group members co-operate to make something beautiful together. Ensure that there is a suitable glue available (eg Copydex).

 Face-Painting

A variety of characters can be created by painting people's faces. Collect together face-paints, brushes and water, mirrors, cotton wool and tissues. Plan your designs beforehand. These can range from clown and animal faces to masks conveying the group's identity, like the Scrap Family who, in the video, all wear a red nose as their symbol of identity – except Belinda who feels 'left out'.

Some tips for face-painting:
* Hold hair back from the face with a shower cap or a baseball hat turned backwards.
* Apply colours using the lightest first, ie white, then other primary colours and black last.
* Keep shapes simple.
* Keep brushes clean.
* Clean hands after using each colour.
* Avoid old-fashioned grease paint.
* Some face-painting kits, available from clown and juggling shops, come with booklets that give design suggestions.

 Quiet Corner

Adults and children can share stories together in a quiet corner. *The Enormous Turnip* would be an appropriate book for this session.

 Jigsaw Pictures

A print of a painting, the more famous the better, is divided into fairly large segments. Each person is given a segment. If there are more people than there are segments, split everyone into groups of eight, or however many segments you have, and use one whole picture for each group. Wheely Bin groups would be appropriate. Players must reproduce their segments of the painting using any type of media that is available (eg crayons, pastels, coloured papers and glue) and in whatever way they choose. If segments are irregularly shaped, people should be given the appropriately shaped piece of paper on which to work. The segments are reassembled into a whole in the same sequence as the original. A fascinating and unique group representation of the painting emerges. Note that each person must work alone, with no reference to or anxiety about the approach others may be taking – any approach is valid. For this reason, the youngest participants can, with support, contribute their own way of looking at something. The finished picture(s) can be displayed alongside an intact print of the original.

 Towns

All kinds of interesting 'towns' can be built using a variety of 'construction materials'. What is needed and how it can be made should be worked out beforehand. Small groups could be given specific responsibilities (eg leisure, public services, housing, education) and time to design their particular section. Everyone then comes together to negotiate the creation of a single town from the perspective of a variety of interests. The construction of the town itself should not start until the negotiations are completed; up to that stage, participants should simply plan together.

 As Many Uses For…

Group members are given pens and pieces of paper. The leader then reads out a list of everyday objects, eg 'A paper-clip, a brick, a disposable nappy, a supermarket trolley…' After each object, the group has three or four minutes to think of as many unconventional uses as they can for it. People may work individually or in pairs and see how many the group as a whole produces. Credit should be given for unusual ideas as well as for quantity.

 Barn/Country Dancing

Someone – a caller with a country-dance band or tapes/CDs – could be invited to come in and teach some traditional dances. As individuals learn and execute the movements they have learned, the group as a whole creates a lovely pattern that constitutes the dance. Looking at film-clips from big Hollywood musicals will help people to see the patterns that can be created by people all moving together.

This activity could be made an extra all-age activity, perhaps with a barbecue or buffet. Children under five will enjoy participating as much as they are able, even if it means bouncing on an adult's knee in time to music.

 Patchwork Quilt

Each person designs and makes a square for a patchwork quilt. Family groups could follow a colour theme. A process for fitting the squares together will need to be worked out beforehand, and the quilt completed outside or beyond the session.

SWEEPING UP

People work in their Wheely Bins for these activities which are designed to help them reflect on the session and make connections with their own lives.

 Prayer Poster

Each person reflects on the session and draws a series of pictures, using stick people, of various aspects of the session that they have enjoyed and through which they have co-operated with each other. They then explain their drawings to the group and paste them onto a large poster headed 'Thank you, God'. The poster is placed in the centre of the group. Everyone hold hands in a circle and one person lead in prayer:

> *Thank you, God, for giving us each other and for helping us to play and work together.*

 Gingerbread Figures

Small figures shaped like gingerbread men (made out of card) are made beforehand and cut into three pieces, as shown. One figure is needed for each person. All the pieces are placed together in a container. One extra-large gingerbread figure is then cut into three pieces and, with fine-tipped felt pens, the following phrases are written on the pieces:

On the head:
* something that the session made you think about
* a time when you are going to need to co-operate
* something you have learned from the session

On the arms:
* something you enjoyed in the session
* something you found hard in the session
* people you worked or co-operated with during the session
* people you trusted and relied on during the session

On the legs:
* a time when you felt really included
* a time when you were on the edge or left out
* what you would like to say to the Scrap Family about their play, or about how they are with one another
* something you would like to tell the group or thank them for

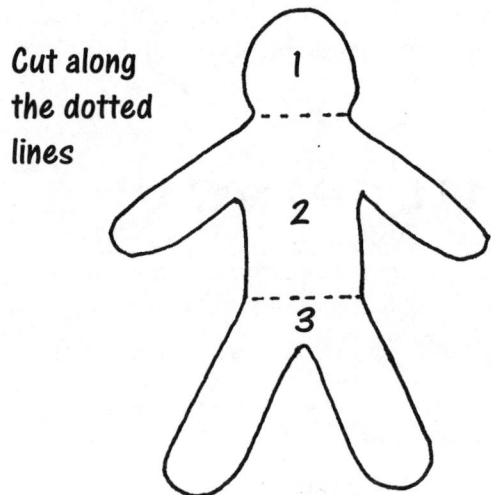

Cut along the dotted lines

The large figure is kept in view. In turn, people take one part of the body from the container holding the small gingerbread figures, and choose what they want to talk about. They are given up to one minute to speak before the next person takes a turn. The object is to collect three pieces to form a whole body, so everyone has three turns. When whole bodies have been collected, the pieces are fitted together and people's names written on them so that they can be identified. Each person should place their figure in front of them. The leader must point out that we are all separate, different and valuable individuals, yet together we make one body, the body of Christ. Everyone holds hands in a circle and says, 'We are the body of Christ.' The whole figures are then put together to form one large gingerbread body shape.

NB The activity will have to be adapted for groups with under-fives in them, perhaps making playdough figures and chatting about the session, what they have enjoyed or learned, and about how important it is to co-operate or work together.

 Acrostics

Together the group form an acrostic of the word 'co-operate', attempting to show what enables good co-operation. People should draw on their experiences of the session. Here is an example:

Communicate clearly
Open to other's ideas
Offer own ideas/gifts
Persevere
Encourage one another
Rely on one another
Affirm one another
Trust one another
Encourage one another

Session 3

REALITY, DREAMS & RUNNING AWAY

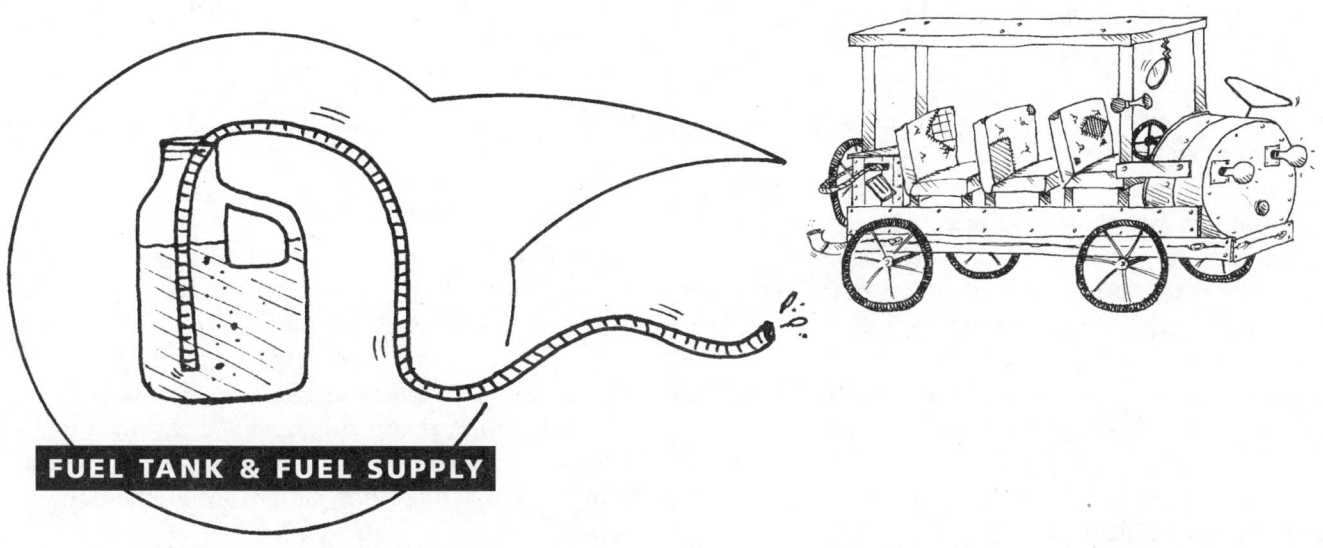

FUEL TANK & FUEL SUPPLY

THE PAPER SKIP

God calls us to dream and to have hopes and visions for ourselves, for each other and for his world. His dream is for each of us to become the person-like-Christ he created us to be, the person who has been largely obliterated through sin – personal, social, global and original. It is healthy to dream, to aspire; yet there is an unhealthy aspect, too. Dreaming may incite us to turn from reality, to pretend that reality does not exist by running away and chasing rainbows. It can cause us to hide and to fear. God gives us dreams so that we can face reality and ourselves, knowing where it is all going, that he is in control and has plans for us.

This session explores our identity, our fantasies and the balance between living in this world and not being of this world. Read, and think about, Jeremiah 29:11–14. Look too at the stories of the hidden treasure and the pearl of great price – Matthew 13:44,45. Our dream must be the kingdom of God, the one thing for which we sacrifice everything else. The difficulty sometimes is to discern what the kingdom of God is in a given set of circumstances! See the story of Joseph in Genesis chapters 37–45 for an example of how God can use dreams to communicate with us.

Facing reality can be a painful business. This session may raise important issues for some, even pain, so be prepared. Have available people who are trained listeners, as well as information that might be useful. See **OK Info 2** for addresses of helpful agencies. Pastoral carers in the church can be on 'stand-by' and information about local resources – people and agencies – made available: Citizens Advice Bureau, counsellors, therapists, social services, contact centres, mediation services, health advice and relationship advice. Throughout this and other sessions, continue to create a tone that suggests that it is OK to ask for help.

A story that has some useful passages for the den-building activities, and is also, ambiguously, about fantasy and reality, is STIG OF THE DUMP *by Clive King (Penguin).*

THE RAG BAG
Underwear

Warm-up games used in this session introduce the themes of hiding and of running away.

 ### Hunt the Thimble

This is a traditional party game. One player leaves the room. The leader hides the thimble (or any small object) and calls the player back in. The player must search for the thimble, guided by the rest of the group who call out whether the searcher is hot (near) or cold (far away).

This is a particularly good game for younger players. It could be adapted to bring closer identification with *Scrap Happy – The Video*. For example, the leader could hide a saucer, normally used for feeding the Scrapyard cats. While the searcher is hunting for the saucer, the other participants indicate nearness or far away by saying 'Meow' loudly or softly.

 ### Hide and Seek

Or any one of its variations.

 ### Kick the Can

This is best played out of doors. The player who is 'It' stands next to a tin can and counts slowly to twenty while everyone else hides. When the count of twenty is reached, 'It' shouts 'Coming!' and goes to look for those who are hidden. As soon as 'It' sees someone, he/she call out that person's name and the place where the person has been hiding. Then they both race back to the tin can. The hidden player tries to reach the can and kick it before 'It' does. 'It' must not guard the can but move away from it while actively looking for the hidden players.

 ### Sardines

Another variation of Hide and Seek. One person leaves the room and goes to hide. The leader allows sufficient time for that person to hide within agreed boundaries, indoors or out, before sending the rest of the group to find the hidden player. As each person finds the hiding place, they silently join the hidden player(s) and hide until everyone has found them. Younger players may best enjoy the game by working with an older partner.

 ### 'What's the Time, Mr Wolf?'

Mr Wolf stands at one end of the playing area with his back to the other group members who are at the other end. At an agreed signal, the group members approach Mr Wolf and call out, 'What's the time, Mr Wolf?' Mr Wolf replies saying any time he likes. This is repeated several times, with Mr Wolf's replies varying, until he suddenly cries out, 'Dinner-time!' The players turn and race for home, and Mr Wolf catches as many as he can. All those who are caught become Mr Wolf's catchers. The game continues until there are no players left. Then others should have the chance to be Mr Wolf.

 ### Circle Chase

Players sit in a circle with the leader outside. They are numbered from one to four or six, depending on how many people are present, so that there are three or four players each with the same number. The leader calls out a number. The players with that number jump up and run clockwise around the outside of the circle, trying to catch the person in front and to avoid being caught by the person behind.

 ### Hidden Halves

The names of various towns or cities are written on pieces of paper, leaving plenty of space between the letters. These are cut in half and separated into piles, with the first half of the names in one pile and the second half in the other. (You may want to sort them into easy and hard names, giving the easier ones to younger players.) The second halves are placed around the room – some may be well hidden, others a little more obvious. As players arrive, give them each the first half of a name, and they must then find the second half. When they have done so, they come back to the leader for another first half. There must be enough for three or four names per player, although there can be duplicates. Vary the difficulty by splitting the name in a more, or a less, obvious place, and even by hiding the first half and giving the player the second.

T-shirts

These games begin to explore the imagination. We all have imagination, even if we don't use it very often. God can use our imagination.

 ## Dream Objects

Each person is given a long, thin piece of paper (30 x 5 cm) and asked to imagine what it might become. They can fold, tear or curl the paper. Each person may have several ideas but can only make one of them. Once everyone has done this, they can show the group what they have made. People will be amazed by the range of imaginative ideas.

This game must be adapted for groups with younger players. In groups of three, players list as many ideas as possible in one minute. Each person makes one item. Then players share in bigger groups of six to twelve, so that people experience the range of ideas.

 ## Quiet Corner

This is an opportunity for space to be given to those who want to be quiet and listen to imaginative stories. Traditional stories such as 'The Ugly Duckling' and 'Cinderella' would be appropriate. Selected reading from *Stig of the Dump* by Clive King would undergird the themes running through this session.

 ## The Dream Game

The leader sends a few people out of the room, possibly two or three of different ages including an adult. He explains to the remaining players that they must pretend they have all had the same dream. The player(s) outside the room have to guess what the dream was about by asking questions that require a 'Yes/No' answer. In fact, when they are questioned, the others simply answer in the sequence 'Yes', 'Yes', 'No'. As the questioners begin, the rest of the group pretends amazement that so much of what they guess is right! If there is a small group of people asking the questions, each of its members should take turns. The game continues until the leader judges that it is about to run out of steam.

 ## One-Word Story Building

The leader asks for four volunteers to stand in a line facing the rest of the group. They must build a story by contributing one word each, starting on the left and then, when the fourth person has contributed their word, the first player carries on, establishing a sequence. The players can say any word they like, preferably whatever comes into their head first, but it must make grammatical sense. Increase the task by asking players to perform an action to go with their word. Both word and action should be performed with enthusiasm! Other groups of four take a turn and the leader should encourage the audience to be appreciative – this will inspire confidence which in turn lubricates the imagination!

 ## Story Building

Players sit in fours and number themselves one to four. The leader gives each group the first line of a story and then calls out a number. The person with that number continues the story, until the leader calls another number. Then the first person stops, even if he/she is in mid-sentence, and the new person carries on, inventing new characters and situations as he/she talks. After everyone has had a number of goes at contributing, the leader calls a new number and instructs the person whose number it is to finish off the story as quickly as possible. The leader must resist the temptation to establish a sequence of numbers, and keep things as random as possible. Examples of first lines are:

* 'Be careful,' said the old lady. 'You nearly knocked me down.' And she…
* Pippa sat bolt upright in bed. 'Oh good,' she thought. 'School holidays…'
* It was raining very hard as Max ran down the street in his swimming trunks…

Trousers

These games encourage players to begin to think about their own identity and its possibilities, and also to stop and take notice of the identity of others.

 ## Who am I? Who are you?

Players sit in circles in groups of six or eight. The leader asks one person from each group to put up a hand. This person will start the activity each time the leader gives him/her the beginning of a sentence. The person completes the sentence for the leader, then the next person to the left in the circle completes it, and so on. All the sentences should give people the opportunity to make statements about themselves. Examples include: 'My name is…', 'My hair is…', 'My eyes are…', 'I like to…', 'I'm good at…', 'I am…' Then the game changes so that people say, 'You are… and you…' about the person to their left in the circle.

Superheroes

The leader cites some examples of superheroes for the group (eg Superman, Batman, Supergran) and explains that they are going to invent some new ones. First, the group can learn the mechanics of the game by each person using their own name. They all stand in a circle, and the leader chooses someone across the circle. He claps once, points at that person and starts to walk towards him/her, saying the person's name as he does so. He should walk fairly slowly. The person the leader has chosen then chooses someone else, but never anyone standing next to them. As before, the chooser claps, points and walks towards that person, saying his/her name. In this way, a flow is set up whereby players walk into the spaces just vacated as the person they have chosen chooses someone else.

As the group gets better, the game can speed up. However, note that, as usual, this is about establishing something together, not about catching anybody out.

Once things are up and running, the leader can explain the next stage of the game. Everyone is to think of a quality about themselves that they really like. They then turn this quality into the name of a superhero, for example maybe they are a good listener and so they become Earman or Listening Woman; maybe someone is good at being a friend and so becomes Superfriend. People should be given time to think before the leader goes round the circle, listening to everyone's superheroes. People are then asked to think of an action to go with their superhero. As with the games in Session 1, people are encouraged to ask for help and other players may not shout unsolicited suggestions. There should be no shame in wanting help at any stage.

The leader goes round the circle again, with everyone giving their superhero an action and doing it. The rest of the group repeats it back to them. The game is played again, this time using each player's superhero instead of their real names.

 'If This Person Was…'

This is best done in groups of up to ten, so players may need to be split into their groups and a leader assigned to each. Each group sits in a circle and the group leader asks for a volunteer. He tells the volunteer to choose someone else in the group without revealing who this person is. Other group members can then ask questions using the following formula: 'If this person was…what…would they be?' and the volunteer must answer. At strategic points, the leader may ask if anyone thinks they know who the person is and, if they make a guess, the volunteer must say whether they are right.

Note that the volunteer does not have to know the person he has chosen all that well. He can do it on an impression gained over the last two sessions. The questions can be about animals, food, holiday, furniture, colours, anything at all (eg 'If this person was an animal, what animal would they be?', 'If this person was a piece of furniture, what piece of furniture would they be?'). The volunteer should try to be as specific as possible in his answers (eg if it is a chair, what sort?).

 Caricatures

The players work in pairs, **A** and **B**. **A** starts off by walking around the room as naturally as possible, greeting people as he encounters them. **B** follows behind fairly closely and copies **A** as exactly as possible. Once satisfied that he is copying **A**, **B** begins to exaggerate **A**'s actions and voice slightly. Then the leader stops what is going on and tells **A** to stand behind **B**. **B** now continues to move around the room and greet people as a slightly exaggerated version of **A**. **A** must try to copy **B**. Once he thinks he is doing this, **A** exaggerates what **B** is doing.

When the leader thinks everyone has reached this point, he tells **A** to carry on and asks **B** to sit down and observe. They are watching all the **A**s create caricatures of themselves! This exercise is repeated with **B** starting, so that all the **B**s end up doing caricatures of themselves. Discuss the experience together. Were there any surprises? How did people feel about exaggerating their own mannerisms?

THE BOTTLE BANK

Brown

The games in this section constitute a (very) light-hearted and safe way of looking in more depth at our identity. What do we do if we can't run away, if we have to find something positive in a situation? How can our imagination help us?

 'Would You Rather…?'

Participants work in pairs, an older person with a younger one. The pairs are grouped to form a circle, and each pair decides on a question to ask the pair to their left. The formula for the question is 'Would you rather…or…?' where either alternative is pretty nasty (eg 'Would you rather eat a plateful of maggots or walk twenty miles in the rain with no shoes on?') The second pair have a few moments only to agree a reply and to explain their answers. They then ask the pair to their left a question of their own.

As before, the leader should encourage as far-reaching ideas as possible and, within the group's boundaries of reasonable taste, get people to offer really horrible alternatives. He could have some cue questions on hand to help players who are struggling to be horrible enough, for example 'What about eating something?' 'What could you mix it with?' 'Where might they have to go?' 'To do what?' 'Who with?'

The 'Glad' Game
7+

Players sit in a circle, or in a number of smaller circles with a leader assigned to each. The leader starts the game by telling the person to his left of a disaster he has just experienced, like 'My house has burnt down'. The second player has to respond by finding something positive in the situation, and say a sentence beginning with the words 'And I'm glad because…'. For instance, in the example given he/she might say, 'And I'm glad because I never liked the wallpaper in the dining room.' The next player to the left then finds another negative aspect of the situation – 'But my favourite books have been destroyed'. And the fourth player adds, 'And I'm glad because I waste too much time reading anyway.' The game goes on round the circle until it comes back to the leader once more.

If there is an even number of players, the leader sits out of the second round so that each person has a turn at saying both negative and positive comments. The group should be encouraged to be as imaginative and outrageous as they want, and to be as ingenious in finding the 'silver lining' as they can. This game also works with the players in pairs, especially linking children with teens or adults.

Story Building
7+

If you have already used Story Building (p 35), use it again, only this time when the leader calls a new number, he must also specify that the player has to follow a certain pattern: for example 'Number two, continue the story and introduce a disaster'; 'Number three, continue the story and bring something good out of the situation'. The story must be allowed to develop for a few minutes before the leader adds any more criteria.

Green

These exercises continue to explore the idea of imagination. They encourage people to think freely about positive aspects of themselves, their desires and aspirations.

Ideal Home Exhibition
3+

This activity can be done indoors or outside. Working individually, in pairs or in small groups (or even a mixture of the three), the players build 'dens' for themselves. They decide what it is vital to have in their den and how they might create it, and decorate and furnish the den to make it as close as possible to their ideal home. People will interpret this at many different levels. They should be encouraged to dream about what their den represents: for example, perhaps someone has chosen a cardboard box to represent a cooker. But, in their dreams, what is the cooker really like?

A variety of building materials can be provided, including lots of junk. 'Home-owners' should be very specific: for example, if a group has used newspaper for curtains, what colour would the curtains really be? Maybe their ideal home is a one-bedroom flat. Whatever they build, they must be prepared to take visitors on a tour, giving a detailed commentary of what they are looking at. The commentary should describe the ideal home as it exists in the builder's imagination, not what people can actually see!

My Dream Holiday 1
3+

If children under five are present, the players may work in small groups. Together each group discusses the most wonderful holiday they can imagine – the place, the climate, the activities, the food and who would be there. Then the group makes a giant postcard to illustrate this dream holiday. Together group members must decide on the messages that might be written on the cards – older members of the group will have to use their writing skills to express messages on behalf of the others.

My Dream Holiday 2
5+

People split into small groups of three or four. Each group discusses each member's ideal holiday. The leader guides the discussion by asking them to talk first about holidays they have enjoyed, how these holidays could have been even better; then the leader asks them to use their imaginations to invent, from the discussion, an ideal holiday for each group member. Where would they go? What would they do? Who would they go with? How long would they go for? Then each person selects one holiday and devises a television ad for it, or a short feature for a

Wish you were here type of programme. Alternatively, the same discussion can be used as the basis for a picture, a collage or an activity involving writing (and designing) a postcard to send to a friend from this ideal holiday. This may be more appropriate, depending on the ages of your group members, or the groups can be offered the choice. The important thing is that people *dream* about their ideal holiday.

5+ Snapshots

The players divide into groups of four or five, and the leader explains that he is going to give them a number of titles or captions for which they must make a 'living picture'. As in Still Images (p 16), the pictures will have no movements and no sound. The actors can represent people or objects. For each title they have a few minutes to discuss and to try ideas. Then the leader claps, blows a whistle or gives a countdown from three, and the players make their group picture. When the pictures have been formed, the leader moves on to the next. When the groups have done six or seven pictures, they could backtrack and look at some of the pictures formed by individual groups, perhaps adding speech bubbles and think bubbles. Some ideas for titles are: 'Wish you were here', 'The dream holiday', 'The perfect family', 'My ideal baby-sitter', 'Home, sweet home', 'When I grow up...', 'This is the life'.

5+ Relative Advertising

As with Dream Holiday (see above), the players divide into groups of four or five. The leader explains that each member of the group has to choose a relative he/she really likes and who is not at the session. The group must devise a one-minute ad for that relative, including a slogan and/or jingle explaining why this person is such a good aunt/brother/cousin. Each group can show a selection of ads to the others. Groups with younger children present may prefer to make a poster of their favourite relatives together.

7+ An Ideal Friend

In small groups (of three or four) each player considers what he/she is like as a friend. What qualities for being a good friend does each have? One member of the group takes notes while people discuss their friendship qualities with each other. The 'scribe' writes down the friendship qualities and, when the group has finished, the 'scribe' reads out what he/she has written. This is the group's 'friendship profile'.

Each group then creates an imaginary 'animal' – a kind of fantastic creature – using the bodies of the group members. This 'animal' must express at least parts – those which the group considers most important – of the group's friendship profile. They have a few minutes to work on their animals. Then the leader sets the animals moving around the room, greeting each other. Some will probably begin to establish relationships with other animals!

Clear

The activities in this section are designed to help people think clearly about themselves, about the reality of their own lives and God's call to them.

3+ Scrap Happy Song

The leader gives out copies of the Scrap Happy Song, and together people look carefully at the words. Everyone, no matter what age, is needed by the rest. Jesus says everybody is the best. No one need be lonely or feel unwanted if we learn to care, share and love one another.

The group sings the song together, and then people talk about the realities. Sometimes we do feel bad about ourselves. We hurt each other – maybe unintentionally, but it still hurts. Sometimes we find it easier to criticise than to praise, to put down than to build up, to see the bad in people rather than the good. Our dream, and God's call, is to live in 'scrap happy' families, groups and communities, where we love, care and forgive one another; where we build one another up and worship God together, recognising that we are not perfect but we can aspire to these ways of being together – with God's help. After the discussion, the group sings the song again, putting in their own actions and movements.

7+ Dustbins

This activity could start with some 'soft' worship – nothing bouncy or triumphalistic but, rather, short and meditative such as 'I'm special' by Graham Kendrick (Kingsway's Thankyou Music, 1986). A large dustbin is placed at the front of the room, and everyone is given a piece of paper and a pen. The leader explains what is about to happen and reassures the group that nobody has to do anything they don't want to. It might help to have music playing quietly during the exercise.

The group are asked to think for a few moments about the things they don't like about themselves; the things that get in the way of a relationship with God; the things that stop them from being the person God wants them to be, the person they dream of being. They write these things on their pieces of paper or draw something to represent them. Then, in their own time, they come to the front and put their pieces of paper into the dustbin. Reassure people that nobody is going to read the pieces of paper, which will all be disposed of. The group sings again, and people remain quiet for a few moments, with the leader encouraging them (and maybe praying from the front) to think and pray in terms of the person God wants them to be in relation to him, to other people, to family and community.

7+ A Guided Meditation

The following passage is read slowly and meaningfully, with silence between the sentences to allow the words to sink in. Most people will probably best benefit if they have their eyes closed. The ideas are based on sections of Psalm 139 and Colossians chapter 3.

Lord,
  Where could I go to escape you?
  Where could I run or hide?
You know me. You know everything
  I do...think...feel.
And you love me, with no strings attached.
Help me to love me too, and to accept me as you do.

Lord,
  You created every part of me.
You know me. You know everything
  I need – physically, emotionally, mentally
  and spiritually.
And you care for me, enough to do something about it.
Help me to care for me too, and to accept me as you do.

Lord,
  You say, 'Go and sin no more.'
I don't need to feel guilty or rotten about myself.
  You love me,
  You care for me,
  And you forgive me.
Help me to forgive me too, and to accept me as you do.

God says,
  'Be glad.
You are loved.
You are cared for.
You are forgiven.
  Have courage to live together in harmony.
Love one another.
Care for one another.
Forgive one another.
  Don't hide from one another.
Rather, talk things through.

Encourage. Affirm. Confess. Forgive. Listen.
Learn from one another and,
  In all you do, worship me.
I am with you.'

This section could end with a celebratory song.

CAN RECYCLING CENTRE

Watch Scrap Happy – The Video Part 3.

3+ OK News 3

Use the **OK News** sheet to communicate the main themes of episode three of *Scrap Happy – The Video*. The questions are discussed as the activity develops. People are split into groups, and each group writes a letter to Belinda.

The second activity helps family members to affirm one another. This can be done at home by the whole family, and in the group if the activity is adjusted to group members rather than family.

3+ Play-Mat

A road play-mat and vehicles are set up (most playgroups possess them), and adults and children drive the vehicles. As they do, the leader asks them to think where they might drive the Scrapmobile. Where could Belinda travel to? Have any of them any idea where she might be?

3+ Pop-Up Puppets

The group make junk-puppets of Scrap Happy characters, which pop up out of appropriate places (eg Belinda from a dustbin, Mr Scrap from a cup of tea, Orlando from a very messy chair). Make the puppets out of lightweight material, like paper. The puppet is attached to one end of a 'spring' made from folded paper. The other end of the spring is secured inside the container.

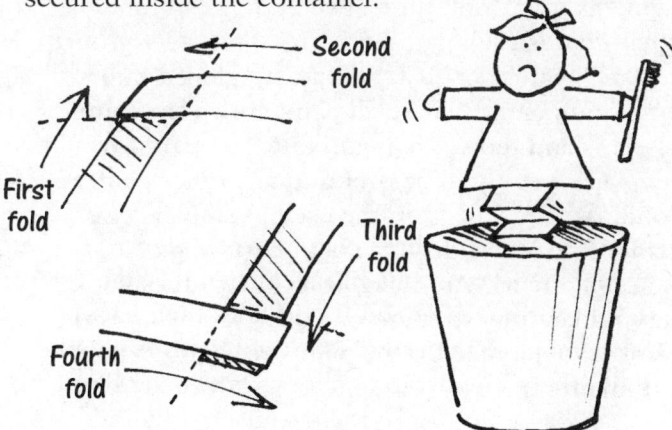

To make the spring you need two strips of paper approximately 80 x 2 cm. Attach these at a right angle to each other at one end, then fold one strip over the other until all the paper is used. Secure the other end of the spring with tape.

5+ Maps and Plans

Games and exercises can be created using maps, plans or public transport timetables. The London Underground map provides plenty of scope – see *Over 300 games for All Occasions* (Scripture Union, 1994) for the game Tube Stations. The group can then talk together about dream destinations. Where might Belinda want to go in her dreams? Where could she have gone in reality?

5+ Puns and Jokes

Like Mr Scrap, many of us enjoy jokes. In teams of four or five, have a joke-telling competition. The jokes may follow a theme (eg 'Knock, knock', names or weather) and each group must think of relevant jokes. When all the groups can say they have at least one joke, they are asked to declare how many they actually have. When all groups have done this, any group can challenge any other to tell the number of jokes they said they had. If a group can really tell that number of jokes, they score that many points and the challenging team loses half that number of points. If they cannot, they lose that many points and the challenging team wins twice that number of points. See how long this can be kept up for. Conditions could be added (eg a joke only counts if it makes at least five people laugh). And why not have an adjudicating panel?

5+ Desert Island Paraphernalia

If you were running away to a desert island, what would you take? Belinda took her toothbrush but forgot about food. Working in pairs, the group draws up a list of everything they would take with them to a desert island and why. They can only take ten items. Gradually the number of items is reduced to eight, six, five, four, three, two and, finally, one. What item is each pair left with? With older groups (ie age 7+) this activity could be developed into a simulation game, where all pairs are on the same desert island though living in different parts. Would one pair's final item be useful to any other pair? Could they benefit from the use of someone else's item? How might they go about bartering or swapping items? Are there other things they could barter, like time, strength or skills? And what is the eventual outcome? Do the pairs create a community or remain separate?

7+ This is Your Life

People divide into groups of six to eight. Each group must write a *This is your life* programme for Nigel in twenty-five years' time. What is his job? Is he happy? Has he got a wife? Children? What have been the significant points in his life? Who have been the significant people? Groups can be as ambitious as they like, and they can make anything true for Nigel. Maybe he has been awarded an Oscar. Maybe he is Prime Minister. Maybe…

7+ This is My Life

People go into groups of three or four and each group is asked to devise an extract from a *This is your life* programme for each group member in twenty-five years' time. Think through the same questions as for This is Your Life. The only stipulation is that the outcome must be positive.

GARDEN WASTE

3+ The Garden of Eden

God's dream for the world was that all should live in harmony with him, with each other and with the ideal home he created for us. This is described in Genesis chapter 1. Sin has prevented us from experiencing that dream in full. However, through Jesus, the dream is and will be a reality (see Colossians 1:20). God's kingdom in all it fullness is God's dream come true.

People have to choose whether to work visually (collage, painting), with words (choral, speaking) or with music (a sound 'collage'). Their choices will separate them into three all-age groups. These groups are allocated leaders who know how to work in each of the chosen media. They then explore together the creation story from the Bible. The group working visually creates a picture or collage; the group working with words practises using their voices to tell the story; and the group working with music composes a musical and percussive account of the creation. You might like to use *The Winding Quest* by Alan Dale; or 'The Drama of Creation' from *A Wee Worship Book*, Wild Goose Worship Group, 1989 (see next page). Finally, all three groups come together to give a unique impression of God's dream for his world and how he intended it to be.

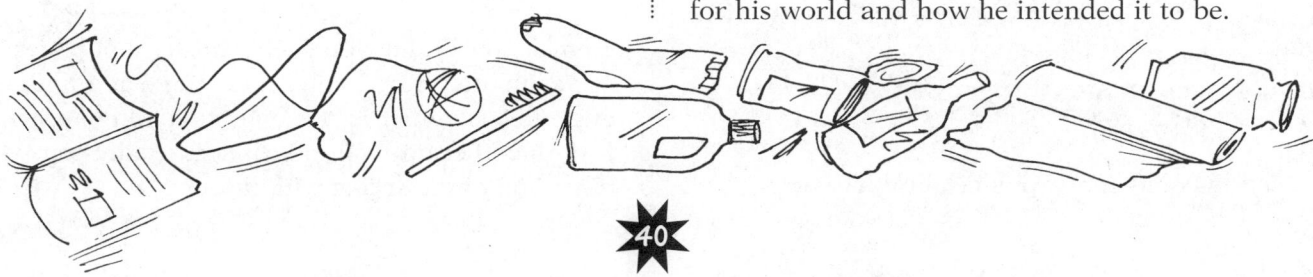

THE DRAMA OF CREATION

In the beginning, God made the world:
Made it and mothered it
Shaped it and fathered it;
Filled it with seeds and with signs of fertility,
Filled it with love and its folk with ability.
All that is green, blue, deep and growing,
GOD'S IS THE HAND THAT CREATED YOU.
All that is tender, firm, fragrant and curious,
GOD'S IS THE HAND THAT CREATED YOU.
All that crawls, flies, swims, walks
or is motionless,
GOD'S IS THE HAND THAT CREATED YOU.
All that speaks, sings, cries, laughs
or keeps silence,
GOD'S IS THE HAND THAT CREATED YOU.
All that suffers, lacks, limps or longs for an end,
GOD'S IS THE HAND THAT CREATED YOU.
The world belongs to the Lord,
The earth and all its peoples are his.

(Copyright © 1989 WGRG, Iona Community, Pearce Institute, Glasgow G51 3UU, Scotland)

The choral-speaking group can be arranged like an orchestra, with the deep-voiced people all together, the low-voiced people all together, and so on. The group must decide which types of voices, or which individual voices, might best express each section of the story. Their tone and speed should be varied to reflect the meaning of the words. Sometimes all the voices can be used together.

The music group will need a range of instruments and, again, they could be arranged as an orchestra. Together they work through the story or drama, and decide which sounds, rhythms and instruments best express each section. Do not be afraid to use silence too.

Members of the collage group must be given time to let their creative ideas flow. Over-preparation should be avoided and the childlike quality of the children's contributions allowed to show. A variety of materials is required, such as fabrics, papers of various sorts, straw, grass, pressed flowers, feathers, shells, printing materials, as well as scissors, pens and glue. People may want to work in pairs or small groups on different parts of a collage once the overall design has been agreed.

JUMBLE SALE

3+ Hunt the Leader

Leaders go out into the local community dressed in a variety of disguises, some designed to blend in, others to be ridiculous (eg a busker, a tramp, a bride and groom outside the church, a businessperson reading a newspaper on a park bench). The rest of the group is split into pairs and each pair given a piece of paper with a list of numbers from one to however many leaders you have – twelve is a good number. Each disguised leader is allocated a number. When players see someone they think is a leader, they must ask him/her a coded question, like 'How green is your jelly?'. If the leader responds in code – 'More red than green' – then the players get that leader to put his/her initial by the relevant number. Players should have a strict time limit, by the end of which they must be back at the venue.

NB People must be paired responsibly so that no pair consists of only young children. It is a good idea to inform the police locally, and to tell leaders to notify the relevant people beforehand, eg the manager of the shop outside which they will be busking. People are usually very co-operative but deserve to know what's going on! The boundaries of the game must be made absolutely clear, for example 'No leader will be beyond XX Street', or 'All leaders will be somewhere on the High Street'.

3+ Pet Show

The Scrapyard Cats feature in episode three of *Scrap Happy – The Video*. People will enjoy coming to a pet show, not one in which you look for the best of breed, but one in which families and households bring along pets to show each other and to share experiences of keeping a pet. Dogs should be on leads at all times, and all animals kept safely in cages, baskets, and so on. People can share pet stories, their habits and tricks, as well as the joys and responsibilities of keeping them. Water and bowls should be available, just in case owners forget to bring drinks for their pets on a hot day. A local vet, or RSPCA officer, could be invited to come and give advice on pet care.

Write to the Royal Society for the Protection and Care of Animals for advice and useful information (eg their Pet Care leaflets) that you could give to pet show participants. A copy of the RSPCA's Educational Resources list may be useful too. Contact your local branch or write to RSPCA, Causeway, Horsham, West Sussex, RH12 1HG; tel (01403) 264181.

SWEEPING UP

For this section, participants work in their Wheely Bins.

3+ Ring Game – Running

Everyone sits in a ring, with the Running Cards in the centre. (See p 43; photocopy/paste these onto card and cut them out.) People pass a running shoe around the ring while music plays. When the music stops, whoever is holding the shoe picks up a card. He/she explains or shows the card to the others, then tells them whether the person on the card is helping to make things better, to improve a situation, or not. If the answer is yes, then that person is in tune with how God wants people to live (ie peacefully). If the answer is no, then the person is running away from situations and from what God wants. Younger children will need help with this part of the game. They should be allowed to show the card so that others can help them answer the question. Some cards are more subtle than others. The leader may want to stop the activity at this point but, if it is appropriate, he can continue in the following way.

When the cards have been used, the leader introduces a large 'think bubble' labelled 'God's Dream: His Kingdom on Earth'. People then paste onto the bubble those cards that speak of God's dream for a world where people live in harmony because he rules.

3+ Prayer

Jesus taught us to pray that God's dream for the world would be a reality: 'Thy kingdom come on earth as it is in heaven'.

The group pray the Lord's prayer together, perhaps using some actions that the younger ones can follow. Eyes are kept open and people stand in a circle. They use the version of the prayer normally said in their church. Possible actions include: looking at each other and smiling while saying, 'Our Father'; raising a hand high for 'Which art in heaven'; sweeping this hand across the sky while saying, 'Hallowed be thy name'. If someone has worked out the actions beforehand and keeps them simple, others will be able to follow. The group may need to practise together first, before praying the prayer with actions.

15+ Reflection

People take up poses to form 'statues' to show how they feel at the end of the session, and add a sound/noise to make their statues more meaningful. In turn, they demonstrate their statues and noises. Music can be played quietly in the background while people think through the following questions:

* What spoke to you from the session?
* Reflect on the reality of your own life now.
* What are the hopes and the good things about your life?
* Are there things that you would like to run away or hide from, but you know need to be faced?
* Is there anything you would like to share with the group?

Paper and pens should be available so that people can jot down their thoughts, and allow time for sharing (but only those who want to). It may be more appropriate for people to share in pairs; the leader should try to be sensitive to the mood of the group. This can develop into a time for sharing information (ie knowledge that any group members may have of local help and support) which the activity brings to mind. If appropriate, this can lead to a time of prayer.

Running cards

Use a photocopier to enlarge the cards, then cut them out to use in **Sweeping Up**.

Mel and Colin have had a quarrel. They are not speaking.

Jenny washed David's knee, which he hurt when he fell off his bike.

Mrs Dean visited Ben when he was unwell, and read him stories.

Mr Smith told a joke when Mrs Smith was anxious and wanted him to listen.

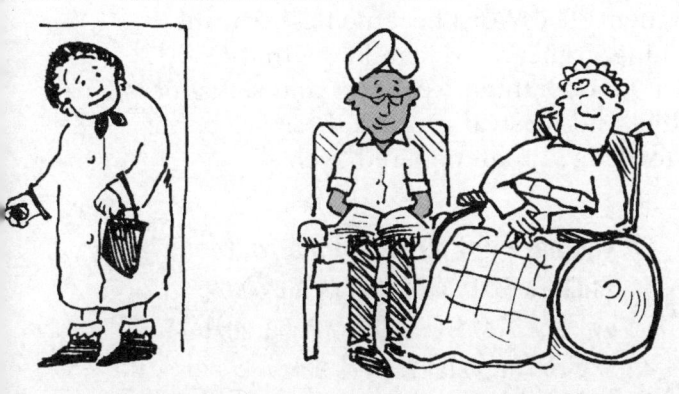

Tom sat with Mr Bell while his wife went to have her hair done.

Sara said, 'That's her problem. It's nothing to do with me!' when Jan lost her purse and bus pass.

Mike said, 'Let's talk about this', when he and Jill were not getting on well together.

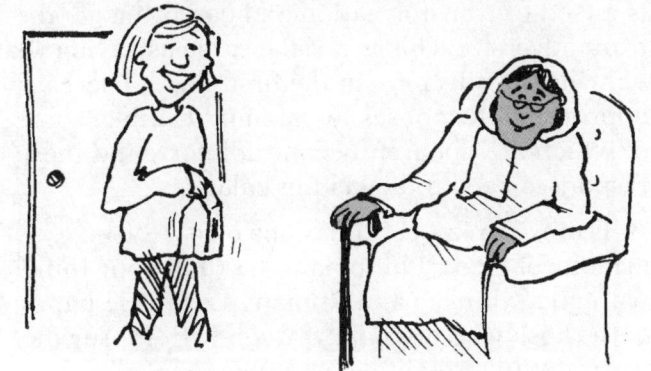

Elaine got Mrs Baker's prescription for her when her knees were stiff with arthritis.

© Copyright Scripture Union 1996. May be photocopied by the church or organisation that has bought this book.

Session 4

ARGUMENTS

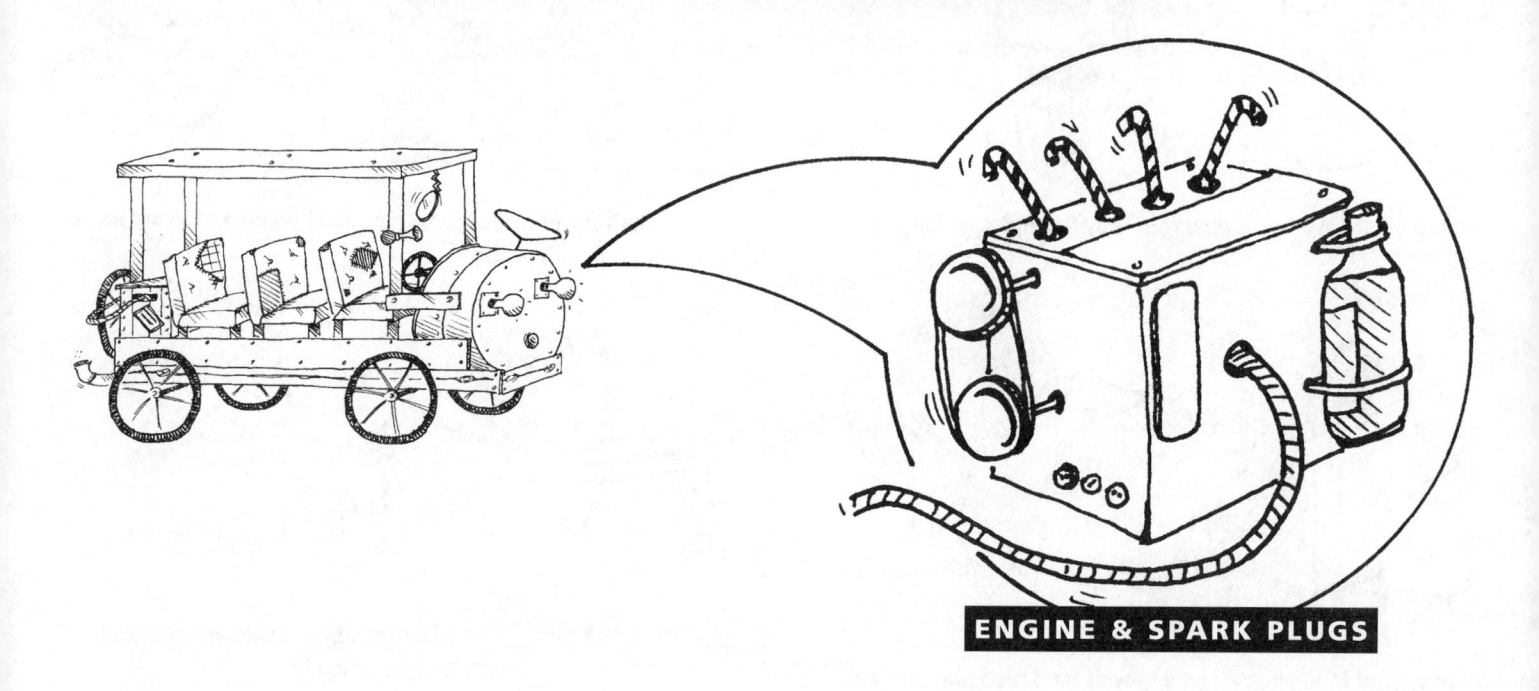

ENGINE & SPARK PLUGS

THE PAPER SKIP

Session 4 is about the reality of life. As Orlando says, life is messy. Participants have so far looked at communication, co-operation and how some things make us want to run away and hide because they do not fit our dreams. This session gives players the opportunity to explore the messiness of life, but does not aim to provide any answers or solutions, rather to acknowledge this messiness as a truth.

Life is not always as we want it to be. Yet God is a God of transformation and can bring good from adversity. This is not the same as saying that he wills the adversity in the first place. There are appropriate responses to pain and trouble, some of which are apparently contradictory, and these responses need to be held in balance.

For example, see Ephesians 6:14–18 (the armour of God), Philippians 4:8 ('Fill your minds with good things') and Romans 12:15 ('Be happy with those who are happy; weep with those who weep'). While retaining an eschatological perspective and protecting ourselves under God's love, we must acknowledge and respect both laughter and tears as real and valid aspects of life. Life in all its fullness cannot be selective; if the statement 'The Word became flesh' means anything, it means we can know that God understands human weakness and selfishness, conflict and frustration, and these are better acknowledged than papered over.

> If you have not already done so, read
> THERE'S NO SUCH THING AS A DRAGON
> by Jack Kent (Blackie/Penguin);
> THE VELVETEEN RABBIT
> by Margery Williams (Anderson),
> especially pages 8–10, the
> section about being <u>real</u>; and
> NOT NOW, BERNARD
> by David McKee (Anderson).

This session can provide an opportunity for participants to talk honestly about their uncomfortable experiences – being angry, having someone else angry with you, feeling left out, and so on. It is vital that the leader handles the session sensitively and ensures that nobody feels unduly exposed or unsafe.

THE RAG BAG

Underwear

These warm-up games involve winning and losing, 'success and failure', 'achieving or not', although at a very superficial level. The group may want to move straight on and save any discussion for later; or they can discuss, after one or two of these games, how it feels to be left out, or caught out, or to win. At some point in the session people should be encouraged to listen to the elderly, the young and others as they talk about feelings of exclusion.

Fonz and Nurd (3+)

Everyone sits in a circle on the floor. The leader chooses someone (**A**) to walk round the outside of the circle, tapping each person as he passes them. With each tap **A** says 'Fonz'. At some point, however, instead of saying 'Fonz', **A** says 'Nurd'. The person who has been tapped (**B**) jumps up and chases **A** round the outside of the circle, trying to catch him before they have both run a complete circle (ie before **B**, the 'Nurd', comes back to his place in the circle). If **A** is caught, **B** takes over, going round the circle, tapping and calling other players. If **A** is not caught, he has another turn. Some under-fives may have to work with a partner, and can sit on their partner's knees when they have run round the circle.

Musical Chairs (3+)

This is the traditional party game. As many chairs as there are players are lined up in two rows, back-to-back, along the room. While the music plays, the players walk in a clockwise direction around the chairs. When the music stops, they sit down quickly on a chair. The leader may ensure that people keep their distance from the chairs by placing an object at both ends of the rows, which the players must walk round. Before the game begins, one chair is removed from a row. The next time the music stops, all but one person will have a chair. This person has to sit on a chair for the rest of the game, thereby rendering it unavailable for the others. The play continues, with more people having to remain on chairs, until there are two players competing for one chair.

Grandma's Footsteps (3+)

A player is chosen to be Grandma. She stands at one end of the room, facing away from the rest of the group who stand along the wall at the other end of the room. When the leader says 'Go', the players start to approach Grandma. The aim is for one person to tap her on the shoulder, thereby becoming Grandma. However, at any point, Grandma may turn around. If she sees anyone moving, she calls out the name of that person and he/she must go back to the starting point (ie the wall).

This game can be made more complex for older players by stipulating that the second time someone is seen, Grandma must call out their name and add a comment about what the person is wearing. For example, the first time she catches someone Grandma may say, 'Jason'; but the second time she says, 'Jason with the green jumper'; the third time she says, 'Jason with the green jumper and the white T-shirt', and so on, adding a new feature each time that particular person is caught. Grandma must get the features in the right order every time, so the game rapidly becomes quite a memory-feat! If she gets the order wrong, the player who was caught replaces her as Grandma, and the game starts again.

Hey, Mr Fisherman (5+)

One player is chosen to be Mr Fisherman. He stands in the middle of the room, while the rest of the players line up against one wall. They say, 'Hey, Mr Fisherman, may I cross the water on the way to school?' Mr Fisherman replies, 'Only if you're wearing a certain colour?' The players ask, 'What is that certain colour?' and Mr Fisherman then calls out any colour he likes. Players wearing this colour try to run past Mr Fisherman and reach the other side of the room without being caught. Those who are caught become Mr Fisherman's catchers. Those who are not caught go on asking Mr Fisherman if they can cross the water. When there is no one left on the original side of the room, the players who have made it safely to the other side must cross back again in the same way as before. The game ends when everyone has been caught.

T-shirts

The games in this section require a little more skill, ingenuity and teamwork, to confound either another team or an individual. Again, how does it feel to be on the spot (eg to be Queenie and not know who's got the ball; or, in Electric Shock, to be holding the string attached to the cotton-reel and for your team to lose)?
This is not an occasion for in-depth discussion, but gently to encourage people to notice how they feel. Are they competitive? Is their tendency to blame themselves or to blame others when things go wrong?

Queenie, Queenie, Who's got the Ball? (3+)

Players stand in a circle. One person (Queenie) goes into the middle and sits in a chair, hiding her eyes.

The leader gives a tennis ball to someone who holds the ball behind his/her back. Then all the players put their hands behind their backs. When everyone is still, the leader tells Queenie to open her eyes and stand up. The group chants one of the following rhymes:

> *Queenie, Queenie, who's got the ball?*
> *Are they old? Are they tall?*
> *Are they young? Are they small?*
> *Queenie, Queenie, who's got the ball?*
>
> *Queenie, Queenie, who's got the ball?*
> *I haven't got it.*
> *It's not in my pocket.*
> *Queenie, Queenie, who's got the ball?*

Queenie has to guess where the ball is. She has three guesses before the whereabouts of the ball is revealed and a new Queenie is chosen. The game can be developed by allowing players to pass the ball around while Queenie is watching. Players can then use bluff tactics to confuse Queenie and to support whoever happens to have the ball.

Keeper of the Keys (5+)

This is a variation of the game described in Session 1 (p 13), to use with older children. The Joker is given a water pistol with which to shoot at the person who is blindfolded.

Electric Shock (5+)

This is a development of Pass the Squeeze (p 13). The leader stands holding hands with two players who each hold another player's hand, and so on, so that two lines are formed down the room with the leader at the top of both. There should be an equal number of players in each line. At the other end, opposite the leader, is a chair or small table. On the table is a cotton-reel with a piece of string attached to it. The last player in the line to the leader's right holds the end of the piece of string. The last player in the line to the leader's left has a (plastic) flower-pot poised over the cotton-reel. The leader squeezes the hands of the players on either side of him *both at the same time*. As soon as a player feels a squeeze – and not before – he/she passes it on. When the squeeze reaches the end of the line, the last players try respectively to jerk the cotton-reel from the chair or to trap it with the flower-pot. The leader keeps score, and may swap players round so that everyone has a go being at the end; teams may also swap sides so that everyone has the chance to be both 'catcher' and 'victim'.

Chair Prisoner (7+)

Players form pairs, and each pair is asked to fetch a chair between them. The chairs are placed in a circle (include one for the leader). One person in each pair sits on a chair (the Prisoner), the other person (the Guard) stands behind his/her partner's chair. The leader also stands behind his chair, which is empty, and starts the game off. The object is to get a Prisoner onto your chair by capturing him from someone else. A Guard whose chair is empty calls out the name of a Prisoner. This Prisoner must get up immediately and sit in the caller's chair. Meanwhile, the person who had been guarding the Prisoner tries to prevent him from leaving by tapping him on the shoulder. When they are not trying to get Prisoners, Guards must keep their hands behind their backs; and Prisoners must sit properly on their chairs. If the chosen Prisoner is touched on the shoulder, he must sit back down in his original chair, and the Guard tries again with someone else. If the Prisoner is not tapped on the shoulder, he becomes the Prisoner of the new Guard, and the Guard he has left behind must capture another Prisoner. This game can develop so that Guards use only eye contact and don't call out Prisoners' names. The whole game should then proceed in silence.

Murder in the Dark (10+)

As the title suggests, this game is played in the dark. Before the game begins, pieces of paper are placed in a hat: there should be an equal number of pieces to players, and all but two of them are blank. Of the two that aren't, one is marked 'M' (for Murderer), the other 'D' (for Detective). Players each draw a piece of paper from a hat. The person who draws the paper marked 'D' is the Detective; he reveals his identity and leaves the room. No one else reveals what is or isn't on their paper. The lights are turned off as the 'party' gets into full swing. The Murderer then taps someone on the shoulder. His victim lets out a blood-curdling scream and collapses 'dead' on the floor. The lights are turned on, and the Detective is summoned back into the room to start his investigation of the crime. By asking people questions about their whereabouts and actions prior to the murder, the Detective hopes to establish who has carried out the crime. Only the Murderer is allowed to lie; everyone else must answer truthfully.

Trousers

These games continue the theme of competition. They also start to emphasise pressure – pressure on the individual not to let the team down, to contribute, to pull their weight, to 'get it right'. How do players feel when they do not? What about when others do not?

Jigsaws (3+)

This activity is for groups with high numbers of under-fives in them, such as parents and children from a playgroup. Two or three fairly familiar puzzles can be provided (eg tray puzzles) with the pieces muddled up. The pieces must be sorted into the right puzzles and into the right positions in the puzzles. The aim is to get them right. Some children will need to experiment to make pieces fit the right way up.

Agility Game (5+)

An empty matchbox is placed behind the rear right leg of a chair. (Use child-size chairs for younger players.) The leader asks for a volunteer to sit on the chair and pick up the matchbox without touching the floor with any part of their body. Three or four players could be playing simultaneously, with teams to cheer them on.

Tug-of-War (7+)

This is literally a tug-of-war contest, with mixed teams of around seven. Use a strong rope. The game could develop so that all players must first stand on one leg; then go back to allowing players to use both legs but, one by one starting from the back, team members let go of the rope and just mime taking part, until eventually the contest is entirely mimed.

Pass the Orange (7+)

Players divide into teams of eight, or go into their Wheely Bins, and each team lines up along the room. Placed at one end of each team is a bucket containing six oranges, and at the other end an empty bucket. The aim is for each team to transfer all six oranges from one bucket to the other, passing them from one person to the next, down the line. Hands must not be used; instead, the oranges are passed under the players' chins. This has very funny results and is also deeply frustrating! If an orange is dropped, it goes back to the beginning.

Alternatively, try passing the outer sleeve of a matchbox, just using noses…

Word Boxing (10+)

Players are arranged in a square (of about 6 ft) around two volunteers. The two volunteers are the Boxers. They are each assigned to a corner and asked to select their 'seconds' who will support them during the bout. Their task is to win the fight, using only words. A team of four judges will award points for each round, thereby establishing a winner. The leader introduces the fight and the two Boxers, and brings them into the ring. They 'fight' by talking as loudly and enthusiastically as they can about a subject the leader has given them, eg the benefits of Asda over Sainsbury's, the merits of lying in every morning, ball-point pens, the existence of dragons, adventure playgrounds, the inside of a ping-pong ball (the more ridiculous the topic the better because the activity is non-threatening). The style of the bouts can be varied so that at times the Boxers are simply talking simultaneously about two completely different things, and at other times they are arguing on different sides of the same subject. Some Boxers may like to choose their own subjects. The length and number of rounds should be decided beforehand (eg three forty-five second rounds). The leader starts the bout and times the rounds. In between rounds, the seconds give advice, suggestions and encouragement. The spectators cheer the Boxers on, and the judges award points at the end of each round. At the end of the fight, the leader announces who has won the overall contest.

THE BOTTLE BANK

Brown

These games are about valuing our individuality including the perceptions and opinions that may clash with those of others. Even if we are in the minority, we have the right to be listened to and the responsibility of listening to others. Nobody is disqualified from having an opinion.

Agree/Disagree (5+)

The leader explains to the group that one end of the room represents the 'I agree with the statement' section, the other end is the 'I disagree with the statement' section, and the middle is 'I do not know' or 'I have no opinion on this'. The rest of the room also has significance, so halfway between the middle and the 'I disagree' end is the 'I disagree, but not strongly' part, and so on. The leader then makes a series of statements. After each statement, players stand in the part of the room that accords with their answer.

THE SCRA...

Mr Scrap **Mrs Scrap**

START START

Instructions

A game for four players. A dice and a counter is needed for each player. Place each counter on the 'Start' squares. Each player throws the dice in turn. Move your counter the right number of squares after your throw. Read what is on the square that you land on, and do whatever it says.

Meeting Squares

If you land on one of these squares, you and the person you 'meet' both take an extra turn, because you have a deep and meaningful conversation together.

You make a cup of tea for everyone. Everyone moves forward one space.

Mrs Scrap is worried, and you listen. You both move forward one space.

You thank Belinda for the cake. You both move forward one space.

You tell the family to stop pretending and be real. They do. Everyone moves forward one space.

You thank Mr Scrap for your red nose. You both move forward one space.

You help the family to prepare for the next play. Everyone moves forward one space.

HO...

You learn that life is messy and help the family to understand this. Everyone moves forward one space.

You give Mrs Scrap a hug. You both move forward one space.

© Copyright Scripture Union 1996. May be photocopi...

P FAMILY GAME

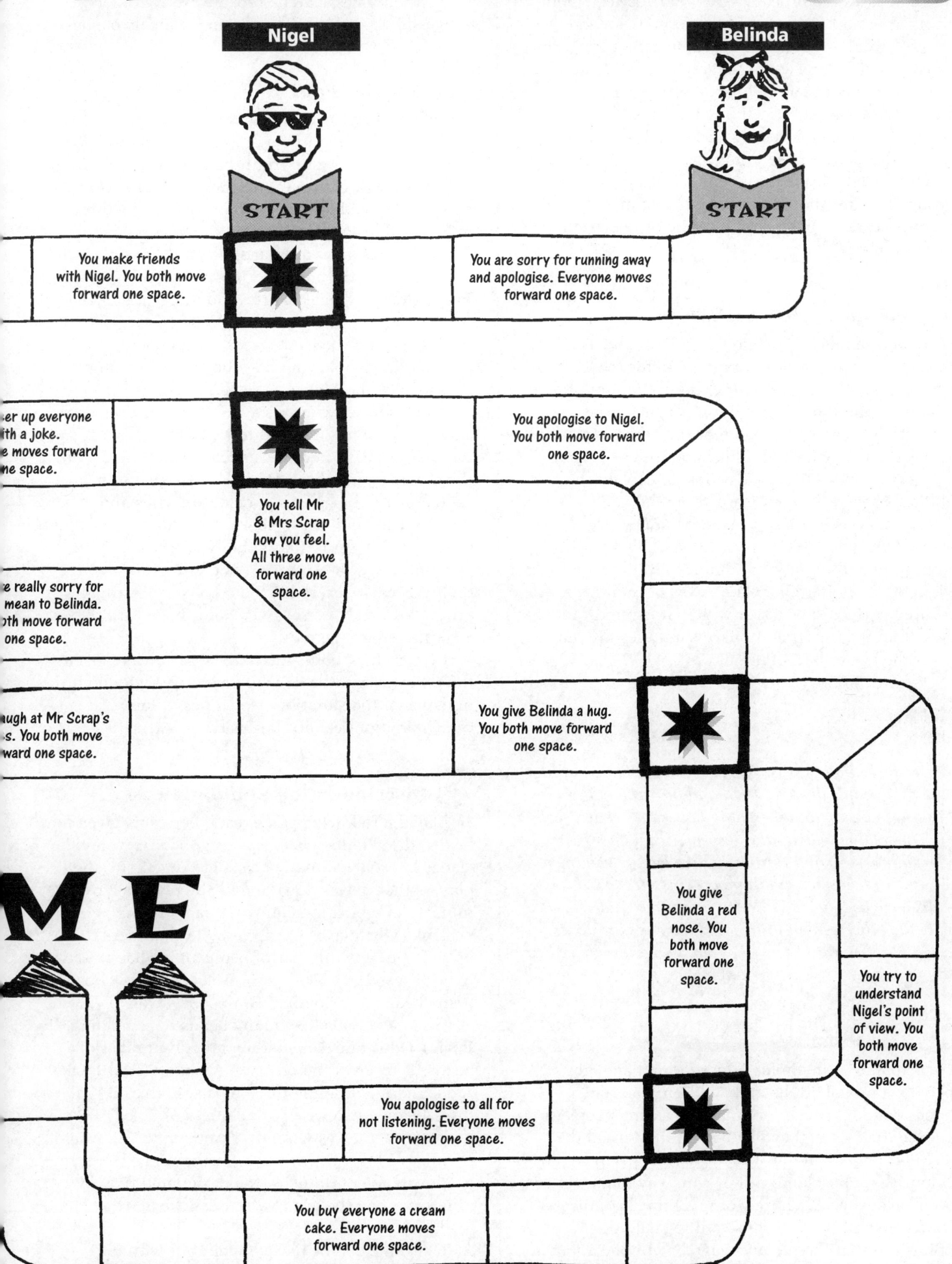

OK NEWS 5

Nigel — START

Belinda — START

- You make friends with Nigel. You both move forward one space.
- You are sorry for running away and apologise. Everyone moves forward one space.
- ...er up everyone ...ith a joke. ...e moves forward ...ne space.
- You apologise to Nigel. You both move forward one space.
- You tell Mr & Mrs Scrap how you feel. All three move forward one space.
- ...e really sorry for ...mean to Belinda. ...th move forward one space.
- ...ugh at Mr Scrap's ...s. You both move ...ward one space.
- You give Belinda a hug. You both move forward one space.
- You give Belinda a red nose. You both move forward one space.
- You try to understand Nigel's point of view. You both move forward one space.
- You apologise to all for not listening. Everyone moves forward one space.
- You buy everyone a cream cake. Everyone moves forward one space.

HOME

the church or organisation that has bought this book.

As the game progresses, the leader asks questions and discusses the process – 'How do you feel about being at the opposite end of the room from your best friend?', '...about being at the same end of the room as your dad?' – and so on. Examples of statements are: 'Take That are a really good group', 'School is worthwhile', ' I get on with my family most of the time', '*Neighbours* is boring', 'Sometimes people ignore me just because of my age'. Trivial statements can be mixed with more serious ones, although peer-group pressure should not be underestimated when it comes to statements about music or television programmes.

Potatoes and Peaches (7+)

Everyone stands in the middle of the room. The leader calls out a series of pairs of items (eg 'Potato or peach') and designates one end of the room for 'potatoes' and the other end for 'peaches'. Players move to one end of the room or the other, depending on whether they feel more like potatoes or peaches. The leader then asks some people to explain their choice. There will be as many different interpretations or reasons as there are people in the room. Other possible pairs include 'Rolls Royce or Robin Reliant'; 'winter or summer'; 'Bourneville Plain or Milky Bar chocolate'; 'eyes or mouth', 'Laurel or Hardy'; 'black or white'. It is important to accept all the interpretations, even if they are not what the leader had in mind.

Green

Part of what allows us to accept the messiness of life (ie that people disagree with and hurt each other) is that we can try to understand how other people feel. The following activities (especially the first two) explain issues and introduce the idea of 'walking a mile in the other man's moccasins'. It's OK if we disagree as long as we listen and try to understand why the other person thinks and feels as they do. If we are to weep with those who weep, we certainly need to learn to empathise.

Likes/Dislikes (3+)

Participants sit in circles of not more than eight people, a mix of adults and children. The leader hands round a packet of Smarties, asking people to choose the colour they like best. Going round the circle, each person tells the rest of the group which colour they chose and, if they can, why that colour is their favourite. When they have all finished, the leader asks those who chose red to stand up. He points out that these players agree with one another, while the rest disagree (they think another colour is best). This is OK. People do not all agree all the time. The process can be repeated using other suggestions, such as TV programmes, pets or toys.

'It's Not Fair!' (5+)

Without telling anyone else, the leader secretly decides on a criteria he will use to distinguish some members of the group from the others (eg all group members with blue eyes). Calling everyone together, he starts to read a story, perhaps one of the three mentioned in **Paper Skip** (p 44). However, before doing this, he gives a Smartie to all the people in the group who fit the chosen criteria. At random points in the story and again at the end, the leader gives out Smarties to the same people. Then everyone stands up, and the leader goes round the group, tapping the people who have been receiving the Smarties deliberately on the shoulder.

The leader now moves away from the group and calls those he has touched to join him. They each get another Smartie, and the leader talks to them so that the others cannot hear. He tells them that they are each going to be given a tube of Smarties and, when he says 'Go', they are to share the Smarties with the others, making sure that nobody is left out. Then, ostentatiously, the leader gives them a tube of Smarties each and sends them back to the main group. Suddenly he says 'Go', and those with the Smarties share them out.

Discuss how both sides – those who were given the Smarties and those who were not – felt about the injustice of the situation. How does unfair discrimination feel, for both sides?

Discrimination Simulation (7+)

To play the following game, each person is given ten beans (dried kidney beans are a good size); only the leader knows how many beans are doled out; the players themselves don't know. The players have five minutes in which to acquire as many beans as possible. One player (**A**) approaches another (**B**), holding out any number of beans in his/her closed hand (it need not be all ten). **B** doesn't know how many beans **A** is holding. **B** must say 'Odd' or 'Even', at which **A** reveals how many beans he is holding. If **B** said 'Odd', and **A** is holding an odd number of beans, **B** receives the beans in **A**'s hand (so if **B** says 'Odd' and **A** is holding three beans, **A** gives **B** the three beans). Likewise with a guess of 'Even'. If, however, **B** guesses wrongly, **B** must give **A** the same number of his own beans as **A** is holding. The game is allowed to continue for the designated five minutes. Then the group discusses the activity together.

The game can be played again but with the following variation. All the players close their eyes, and the leader gives a small number of them a white bean each. He tells them to keep their white beans hidden, then asks everyone to open their eyes. All the players start with ten beans, as before. But this time all transactions must be done on the understanding that if a player has a white bean, he/she can demand to know how many beans the other is holding before deciding to say 'Odd' or 'Even'. If a player with a white bean demands that you play, you must! This is blatantly unfair and gives the players with white beans a tremendous advantage. At the end of the game discuss how the group felt about this version of the game. Were any players with white beans uncomfortable about their power?

Agony Aunt (10+)

A number of letters to the problem page of a magazine are prepared beforehand. Players divide into groups of four, and each group is given a letter. There are examples opposite to start you off. The letters should be humourous but dealing with real life issues (eg sibling rivalry). You could, if you wish, write them as though from characters in *Scrap Happy – The Video*, dealing with the situations that arise in the video. The letters should contain the essence of a situation, not details of how the writer is feeling.

Each group decides on two people to be the writers of the letter, the other two are the Agony Aunts. While the Agony Aunts write a reply, the letter-writers must write a diary entry for the day they wrote the letter. It is here that feelings are expressed freely. After 10–15 minutes, the group finishes their task and swap papers, so that the letter-writers receive the Agony Aunts' advice, and the Agony Aunt receives further insights into the writers' feelings.

Afterwards, the groups discuss the exercise together. How helpful was the advice? Had the Agony Aunts really understood the problem? How does it feel to be understood?

Agony Aunt Letters

Dear Agony Aunt,
I like my room how it is. It's my muddle, but Mum's always nagging me to keep it tidy. Yesterday she barged in, nearly fell over my skates and was furious. It was so funny, but she didn't think so. Instead I got another dose of nagging.
It's so wearing!
Jade, aged 12

Dear Agony Aunt,
The dog came home with a black nose and a marigold hanging out her mouth. She's not allowed out of the garden but the children left the gate open – yet again. (They prop it open to get their bikes out.) Our neighbour is not going to be happy when he sees his flower bed. And I'm not happy with the kids' behaviour. What can I do to make them more responsible?
A perplexed Dad

Dear Agony Aunt,
My sister says it's not fair and she's not speaking to me. She was thirteen when she got her first pair of Nikes and I was only eleven when I got mine. She says I always get my way and she never does. I don't think she's right. What shall I do?
Worried sister

Dear Agony Aunt
I'm over eighty years old and can't get out much, especially in the winter. Sometimes I'm alone all day. I would enjoy getting to know some younger people but am afraid they would not want to spend time with an old woman. What do you think? How could I meet them?
Housebound

Clear

The exercises in this section are about empathy, but also about beginning to understand that different people's emotions are energised by different things – yet more fuel for the messiness of life. Something which makes me angry, which I think worth arguing about, might be completely insignificant to someone else.

Detectives (3+)

While the under-fives play in parent and toddler groups and playgroups, players can observe them. Watch for causes of conflicts. How did the children resolve conflicts – fighting, retreating, talking, negotiating? Or did a third person arbitrate? How might some of the conflicts be prevented? The adults discuss what they have seen and whether or not the children handled situations well.

Observers should stay out of child-child conflicts unless someone is getting hurt. Any intervention should be done in such a way that the children resolve the conflict themselves. They should be helped to find their own solution rather than have one imposed on them.

Reverse Roles (5+)

Props are provided to enable some drama situations to be played out in pairs. The more powerful roles are assigned to children and the other roles to adults (eg a child takes the nurses role, and an adult the role of patient). Act out some of the following, or similar, scenarios:

1. The patient has fallen and hurt an arm. A nurse examines the patient, asks questions, bandages the arm, and so on.
2. A teacher helps a pupil to read.
3. A policeman questions a youth who is suspected of stealing.
4. A parent and a child get ready for school.
5. A school-crossing patrol person helps children to cross the road.
6. A football coach encourages a player in his/her team.

Exciting/Boring (7+)

People split into pairs and each pair holds a conversation by repeating opposing statements: **A** says, 'It's exciting' and **B** says, 'It's very boring' again and again. The tone, speed and pitch of voice in which they say their statements should vary. This continues for about one minute, then the pair can move on to other topics, eg 'It's raining/The sun's shining', 'Red is best/Blue is best', 'A fork is more important/A knife is more important'. There are no 'winners'.

Role Plays (7+)

The leader asks for volunteers to role-play two or three scenarios (two volunteers for each scenario). The volunteers are each given the instructions for their roles (see p 57). If reading is a difficulty, the leader can whisper the role and any other necessary information to the appropriate player. Then he explains the situation to the rest of the group, but doesn't give away the role instructions – he just sets the scene and asks the group to observe what happens.

The players are given time to get into role. The role play should last for a reasonable length of time, then the players stay in role while the rest of the group make their observations. How did each player react to the other? What excited each of them? Were there right and wrong answers? They can ask questions of the role-players. How did they feel, especially about the outcome? During this time, the role-players are addressed in role and given the opportunity to say how they feel. After a while the leader asks them to come out of role, say their own names and shake hands with their role-playing partner. They can then join the rest of the group in discussion. Was the argument settled? Did one person 'win' or were both satisfied with the outcome? A resolution that is satisfactory to both parties is a 'win-win' outcome and is the best one to aim for.

'Things That Make Me Feel...' (7+)

Players sit in the middle of the room. The leader calls out an emotion (eg 'Excited!') and each person thinks of something that makes them feel this way. The leader asks for at least two, but not more than five, volunteers. These people, in turn – or simultaneously if the group is big enough – take thirty seconds to tell their listeners what it is that makes them feel excited. Each volunteer should be listened to by a number of people, and he/she must be as loud and as passionate as possible. The people around the volunteers must listen and support them noisily and with body-language. They must not interrupt but simply encourage and accept what the speaker is saying, perhaps by agreeing – 'Yes, you're right!' Examples of feelings are: feeling important, feeling special, feeling that I matter, feeling part of a group, feeling clever, and so on.

If the group can deal with it, move on to more negative emotions (eg feeling left out, scared, lonely, embarrassed). Again, the support of the people listening is very important.

CAN RECYCLING CENTRE

Watch Scrap Happy – The Video Part 4.

OK News 4 [3+]
Use the **OK News** sheet, especially with groups which are not using the video. Tell the story, look at the pictures, and discuss the questions.

Treasure Hunt [3+]
In groups of three or four, players hunt for treasure and create messages. One or several short treasure hunts can be devised using themes from the video, such as 'Life is messy', 'We need each other', 'Life is a journey', 'God loves us all', 'Jesus is our friend'.

Each group is given a message on a strip of paper in upper and lower case writing. A designated area in which to work and a time limit are agreed. Each group then scavenges for items beginning with the first letters of the words in their message. They then arrange the scavenged items to make the message.

Masks [3+]
If you have not already done so, why not try making masks or puppets which have two sides? See **Scrap Art Info 3** and **4** for mask-making and puppet-making ideas. One side of the mask depicts the public face worn by the characters in the video and the other side shows the more private face. The masks can be used to express words and phrases that each character might use according to their different moods.

If appropriate for the age groups present, the masks can be used to change what happens in the video. For example, start Kitty and Orlando arguing with their angry faces, then stop the action and turn one mask around. What difference does it make?

Song Time [3+]
Use the Scrap Happy Song, the Scrap Cat's Chorus and 'Dem bones' (pp 92–94) to explore some of the themes in *Scrap Happy – The Video*.

Film Characters [5+]
Each person talks about his/her favourite films and film characters. People can paint, draw or make collage pictures depicting the scenes showing their favourite character. Then, in turn, they show artwork to the rest of the group and explain why they particularly like that film, which character they identify with most and why. The group should be encouraged to listen to and appreciate different viewpoints.

God Talk
Belinda listened to Kitty and discovered that God loves us all and Jesus is our friend. Nigel listened to Orlando and heard that God's love is always with us. Kitty and Orlando may argue, but they agree on some things!

In their Wheely Bin groups or those of similar size and with mixed ages, group members are invited to think about and share some of the times when they have been especially aware of Jesus' friendship or of God's love for them. There can be great value in listening to each other's testimonies but people should keep their stories short. Some may be comfortable just listening – and this is fine.

Now choose one of the following three games:

1 God With Me [3+]
Teach young children the actions so that they can join in even if they are unable to read the words.

> *God is with me in the good times.*
>   *(Thumbs up)*
> *When I'm happy, so is he.*
>   *(Smile)*
> *God is with me in the good times.*
>   *(Thumbs up)*
> *That's because he cares for me.*
>   *(Point to self)*
> *God is with me in the bad times.*
>   *(Thumbs down)*
> *When I'm sad, he won't let go.*
>   *(Cross arms across chest)*
> *God is with me in the bad times.*
>   *(Thumbs down)*
> *That's because he loves me so.*
>   *(Point to self)*
>
> (From *A Church for All Ages* by Peter Graystone and Eileen Turner, Scripture Union, 1993)

2 Cat and Dog Fights [7+]
The leader ascertains who in the group owns pet cats and dogs. He then asks them to suppose that they own a cat and dog who both have a tendency to fight. What would they do to stop them fighting? The group members then discuss the various

solutions, like throw some water at them, divert their attention, keep them in separate rooms.

Kitty and Orlando were arguing (almost fighting). We might say that they were having 'a cat and dog' fight. Together, the group makes a list of tips that may help Kitty and Orlando not to fight or argue so much in the future, eg 'Count up to ten', 'Listen to one another', 'Check that you have really heard what the other has said', 'Tell each other how you feel'.

10+ 3 Psalm 23

Recognising that God loves us all and is with us in the various circumstances of life, people are asked to listen and reflect on their own lives while Psalm 23 is read from a modern version of the Bible. The person reading the psalm should read meaningfully, pausing briefly at the end of key phrases and verses. The last verse should have particular emphasis.

15+ Journeying

Orlando sees life as a journey. The leader asks each group member to consider his/her life-journey and draw a graph to show the major high points and low points. This may have to be limited to a certain span of life (eg the last five years). In small groups, each person shares some of the major high and low points. They need share only what they want to and at a level they feel comfortable with.

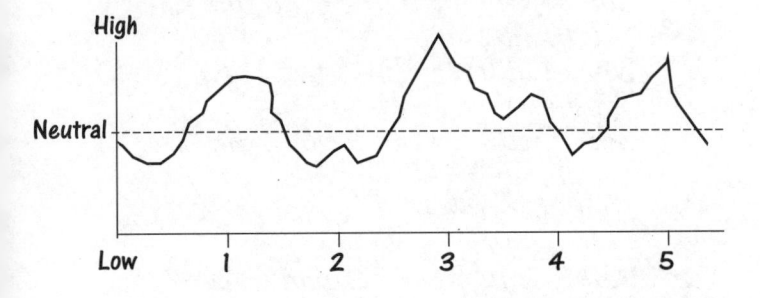

GARDEN WASTE

7+ Wide Game

People may well need to let go of some positive energy, since this session can be fairly intense or a little bleak! This game could be as simple as a straightforward water fight (wonderful for releasing tension!) or more complex like the following suggestion.

The group divides into three or four fleets, each with an Admiral and a Quartermaster. A fleet has a base where their Quartermaster sits, and each fleet has Battleships, Submarines and Destroyers in the proportion 1:2:3 respectively. The players are each told what type of ship they are (a Battleship, Submarine or Destroyer) and given a piece of coloured wool to denote the fleet they belong to (each fleet being a different colour). The wool is tied around the player's wrist, but not in a knot that is too hard to untie. The battle rules are that a Battleship wins over a Destroyer, a Destroyer wins over a Submarine, and a Submarine wins over a Battleship.

The leader gives a signal, and all the ships sail to a central battle area. If there is the space, the battle area could be a fair distance from the bases. For a battle between two ships to take place, the players must 'tag' a player from another fleet in order to challenge them. Each player then says what ship they represent. If they are the same, nothing happens. But if they are different, one player will resign his/her wool according to the battle rules. The defeated ship has to go back to base for a new piece of wool, whilst the winner returns to base to give the captured wool to the Quartermaster.

Players should eventually be able to work out which ships the other players are and start to target their challenges while remaining on the look out for their own pursuers. There could be a half-time when players are reassigned ships. The team with most pieces of captured wool wins the battle. No player can continue without a piece of wool. Quartermasters are in charge of wool supplies. Admirals co-ordinate their team's tactics, as well as ensuring that other teams are not cheating.

3+ Other Games

If there is not the space or numbers for a wide game, choose any game from the *Underwear* section of any session. These can work as tension-releasers, but probably something physical would be best.

JUMBLE SALE

3+ Messy Afternoon

Participants must be warned beforehand to wear old clothes. Arrange a session in which all ages can participate in messy activities. Ideas might include:

1 Finger-painting which may turn into hand-painting.
2 Foot-painting – trays of shallow paint that people walk through and then over lengths of paper, leaving their footprints. Be sure to arrange for foot-washing facilities too.
3 Cover a wall with paper and protect the floor with ground- or plastic-sheeting. Throw sponges

dipped in paint at the paper on the wall; spray the paint (water-colours in spray containers) or flick it off brushes; try a variety of old paint rollers and balls of rag. Just experiment.

4 Provide clay, modelling boards and tools, and protect surfaces with sheeting or newspaper. Encourage people to experiment. Some may want to play with the clay, while others might try making tiles or coil pots.

5 The group can experiment with making models or collages out of different sorts of junk which is stacked up in piles or put into skips. Ensure that sufficiently strong adhesive is available for people to use.

6 Provide old scrap mechanical objects (eg clocks, watches, some toys and gadgets) which are safe enough for people to take apart. Together, the group can look at the various bits and pieces – their shape and purpose, then re-use the parts to make something new (eg a metal collage on thick, coloured card, a model or mobile).

7 Have a water-fight using water-spray bottles, buckets and hose pipes.

NB See **Scrap Art 1** and **2** for further information.

Include everyone in the process of clearing up towards the end of the session. This is extremely important. It is all right to make a mess, but it is also necessary to clear up afterwards.

Bicycle Maintenance and Riding

Beforehand, arrange for cyclists, old and young, to bring their bicycles and tool-kits, and hold a session on bicycle maintenance, including regular cleaning, servicing (nuts, bolts, screws), lubrication, tyres, lights and brakes. Enough young people and adults who are knowledgeable about bicycles should be on hand to help and advise while the cyclists actually service their own vehicles. Also have available spare tools that may be necessary.

> A range of useful leaflets and information may be obtained from The Royal Society for the Prevention of Accidents, Cannon House, The Priory, Queensway, Birmingham, B4 6BS. A bicycle guide giving detailed information about maintenance, is available from RALEIGH, c/o Consumerlink, PO Box 362, London, SW11 3UD.

Once the cycles have been serviced, the cyclists can practice their cycle manoeuvres like riding in a straight line without wobbling, riding in a straight line very slowly, riding around obstacles and corners, signalling. The local Cycling Proficiency Officer could be invited to work with both adults and children to improve their cycling skills.

A Highway Code for Young Road Users gives valuable information and illustrations about riding safely on the road. It could form the basis for a fun quiz. People divide into two groups, **A** and **B**, and each is given copies of *A Highway Code for Young Road Users*. The groups must each formulate ten questions to ask the other – **A** asks **B** a question, **B** asks **A** a question, and so on. The groups continue to ask each other questions alternately until all the questions have been asked. The leader then counts up how many each got right.

NB All parts of a bicycle are important and necessary if it is to work properly and be safe to ride.

Balloon Debate

People sit in a circle with three volunteers in the centre. The players have to imagine that the three in the middle are flying over the North Sea in a balloon. However, they are having difficulty keeping the balloon in the air. The only way to keep the balloon airborne and to make a controlled, safe landing is for one person to jump overboard so that the other two may be saved. The volunteers discuss and negotiate why each of them should or should not be the one to jump overboard. Give them time to think themselves into their roles. The three people in the balloon are:

1 A pop star – the lead singer in a famous band with millions of fans – who is due to perform at a concert tomorrow.
2 A parent of three young children for whom the balloon ride was a birthday gift from the family.
3 An experimental farmer who is researching new ways of growing crops in parts of the two-thirds world – the work may well result in saving many starving people.

The people in the circle observe and share their observations at the end. The volunteers must be given time to come out of role and share what it felt like to be involved in the debate.

SWEEPING UP

Guided Reflection

Each person is given a piece of brightly coloured tissue paper or thin paper cut into a diamond shape, approximately 30 x 20 cm. The leader explains that the paper is diamond-shaped to remind us that each of us is a valuable person, just as a diamond is valuable.

People carefully fold their diamonds from corner to corner, both ways as shown opposite. While music is played quietly, the leader explains that he will suggest something about the session for people to think about. When they have thought, they tear a small piece of paper from a folded edge of their diamond. (The leader will need to demonstrate how to do this.) There could be five or six points for reflection, using key ideas that have arisen in the session. Start with an easy one. After each suggestion, time should be allowed for people to think and tear a piece from one of the folded edges of their diamonds. Younger people may participate at the level of tearing the paper to make a pattern.

Suggestions for reflection are:

* An activity you enjoyed
* Someone you got to know a little better today
* A time when you felt left out
* A time when you felt included
* Something you have discovered in the session
* Part of your life-journey that you are glad about
* Part of your life-journey you found difficult
* What you would like to say to Orlando and Kitty today
* An argument you have had
* How you react to arguments
* Someone you need to talk to, to sort out a difference
* Something you would like to do as a result of today

The tissue paper should end up with a series of pieces torn out of the folded edges. The players carefully open out their tissue paper and look at the pattern they have created. Note how each pattern is different and unique as we are, and how through each of them runs a cross – a reminder or symbol of God's love for us.

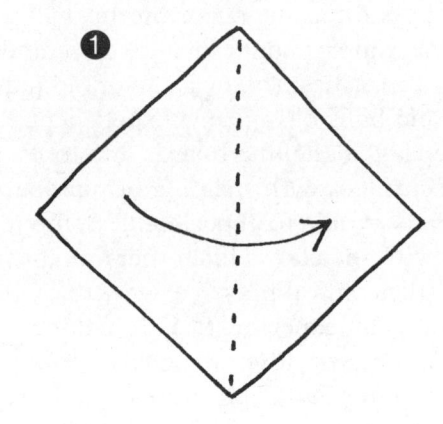

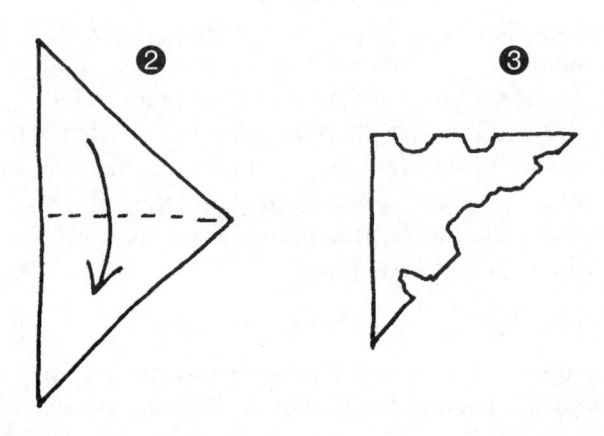

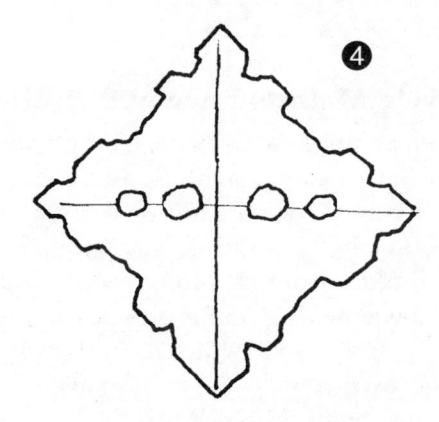

Each group member in turn is given an opportunity to share one of his/her thoughts and/or feelings that occurred while doing the exercise. It should be made clear that to 'opt out' of the talking is all right, though everyone needs to listen. After the discussion, have a short period of silence, giving people the opportunity to bring their thoughts to God.

Conclude with the Scrap Happy Song.

Role plays

1 *Scene:* A brother and sister, Tom (aged 12) and Gill (aged 8), at the breakfast table. Their parents have suggested a family outing to the cinema on Saturday. It is Gill's turn to choose the film.

Tom: You don't want to go to the cinema because there's a football match, and because you know it is your sister's turn to choose the film. She likes soppy Walt Disney films like *The Little Mermaid* and *The Lion King*. You prefer action packed 'Indiana Jones' films – they're the best. So you argue with your sister.

Gill: You are excited about going to the cinema. It is your turn to choose and you know there's a good Walt Disney movie on – they're your favourites. You are excited and convey this to your brother, letting him know which film you want to see. An argument develops between you.

2 *Scene:* Jack (aged 67), and Elaine (aged 27) have been asked to choose the hymns/music for Sunday's service. They have a difference of opinion over the types of music to include.

Elaine: You like modern hymns and songs with a swing to them, the sort that make you tap your foot or clap. You believe that these are the best and everyone will benefit from them. You expect Jack to agree and to choose your type of music only.

Jack: You value some of the old hymns and have recently discovered Gregorian chants and Celtic music for worship. You do value some of the 'new' church music, but it still feels quite old in style compared with the music your grandchildren listen to. You feel strongly that a range of music should be included in a service to reflect the preferred styles of the range of people in the church.

3 *Scene:* Backstage at the Scrap Theatre.

Belinda: You want to wear a red nose for the Scrap Family play. You do not have a speaking part, but feel that you want to belong and be as important as the others in the play. You tell Nigel that you want a red nose.

Nigel: You are a proud actor with a speaking part. You think Belinda is less important than you: she doesn't have a speaking part and shouldn't wear a red nose like the more important actors. You argue with Belinda.

4 *Scene:* Orlando and Kitty at home in the Scrapyard.

Kitty: You like to be neat and tidy. Your part of the Scrapyard is always tidy. Orlando makes you angry because he is so untidy. Today he has left his clothes strewn on the floor. You suggest to Orlando that he tidies up his clothes.

Orlando: You are easygoing and happy with mess and untidiness. Your sister Kitty is the opposite. She likes to be neat. You get angry when she keeps telling you to tidy up. Today you have left your clothes strewn on the floor.

© Copyright Scripture Union 1996. May be photocopied by the church or organisation that has bought this book.

Session 5

PIECING IT TOGETHER

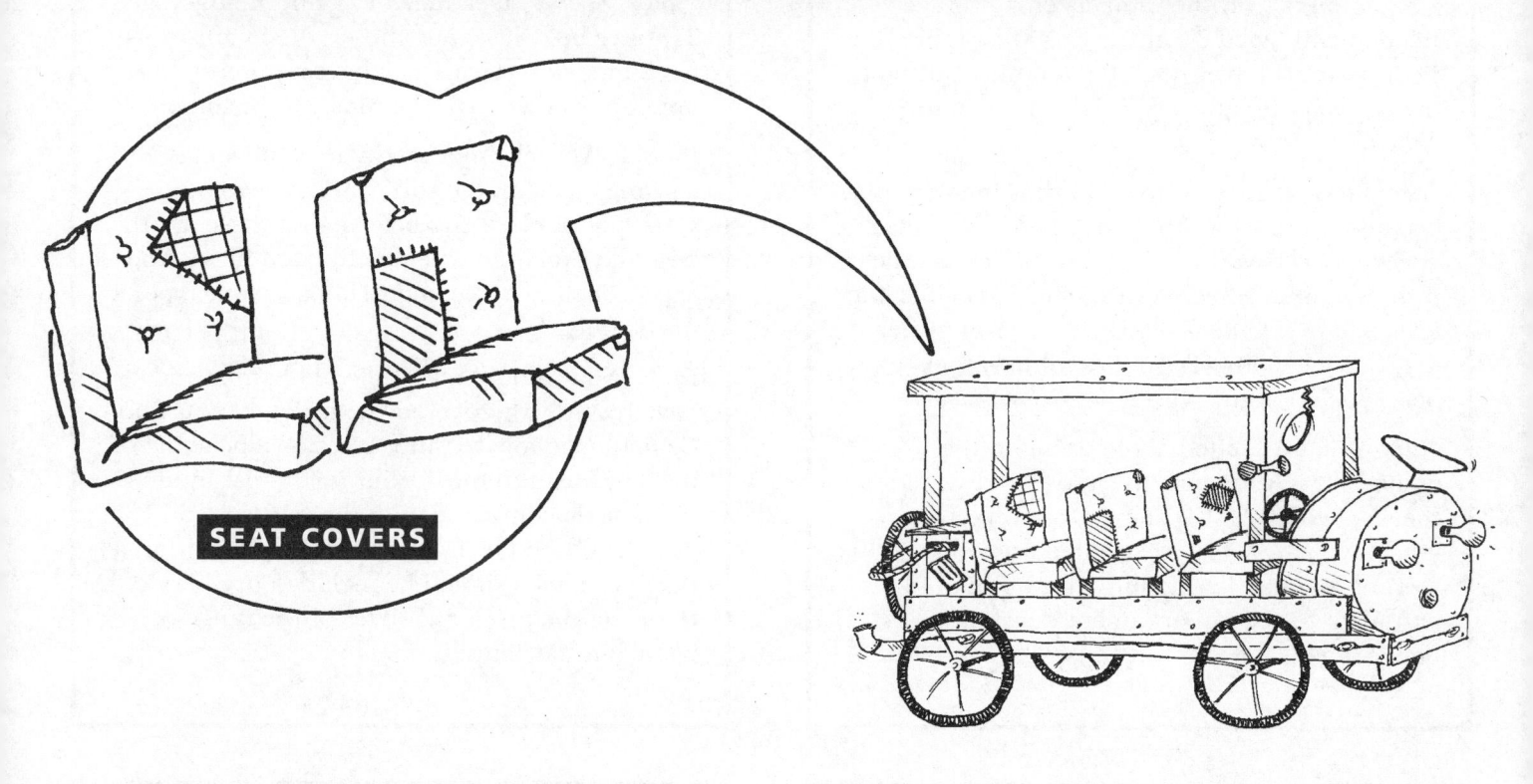

SEAT COVERS

THE PAPER SKIP

This final session is a culmination of the previous ones, completing an exploration that brings us back to where we started – communication, and celebrating how each individual can join with others to create a community that reflects God's diversity and extravagance.

Following on from the previous session on adversity and argument, we now focus on the necessity of differences. How disempowering it would be for us all to be the same. Just as a clock needs many different and complementary components – some more showy than others – so also do we need the less obviously valuable bits of ourselves and of other people. Look at Psalm 139 to see how important our idiosyncrasies are to God. In fact, they are built in by design! He has called each of us by name (Isaiah 43:1) – we are not part of a 'job lot' whose members all share a uniformity.

See also WONDERFUL EARTH by Nick Butterworth and Mick Inkpen (Hunt and Thorpe) for a beautiful celebration of the creation of which humankind is the pinnacle. Two books from Scripture Union that may be useful for groups with younger children are MILES AND THE COMPUTER by Taffy Davies and EMMA by Christine Wright.

THE RAG BAG

Underwear

These are simple warm-up games that set an atmosphere of relaxed fun. The aim is that people enjoy themselves!

3+ Follow My Leader

The group splits into teams of around eight that line up in rows, each with their own leader. This person leads the rest of his team around the room, moving in specific ways and making specific actions; the team must follow the leader in front as closely and as accurately as possible. If two or more teams are playing at the same time, some interesting snaking results! Teams may move outside if there is the space and the weather. On a given signal, the person at the front moves to the back, and allows someone new to be the leader.

3+ Farmyard Frolic

People split into teams of four or six, each of which designates a leader and chooses a farmyard animal. Make sure there is no duplication. A number of buttons, beans or even Smarties are hidden around the room, and team members look for them. Each team leader sits on a chair at the end of the room. When a team member – or a pair if younger children are involved – finds a button, he/she makes the noise of their team's animal, and the leader goes to pick up the button. No gesticulating or other noises are allowed! Set a time limit and after that time, or when all the objects have been found, count how many buttons each team has collected.

5+ Hey, Harry

The group sit in a circle. The leader turns to the person on his left (**A**) and says, 'Hey, Harry!' **A** replies, 'Yes, Harry?' The leader says, 'Tell Harry.' **A** turns to the next person in the circle (**B**) and the dialogue continues. **A** says, 'Hey, Harry!' **B** says, 'Yes, Harry?' **A** says, 'Tell Harry.' **B** turns to **C** and says, 'Hey, Harry!' **C** says, 'Yes, Harry?' **B** says, 'Tell Harry', and so on. This carries on all the way round the circle. When everyone has got the hang of it, the leader introduces the fact that if anyone makes a mistake or hesitates or stumbles, he/she becomes 'One Spot' rather than 'Harry'. If someone who is 'One Spot' makes a mistake, he becomes 'Two Spot'; another mistake and he is 'Three Spot', and so on, up the scale. This has implications for those around them, who must refer to them as 'One Spot' (or 'Two Spot', 'Three Spot', etc) and not 'Harry'.

T-shirts

Teams are about working together. Each member of a team is important, and their contribution should be valued. In Team Call, everyone is a potential winner; in Happy Families, equality is guaranteed since all the assigned characters have equal status in the game; in Cat, Mouse, Elephant, the leader should emphasise that the youngest and quietest players could be asked to decide what the whole team is going to do.

3+ Human Happy Families

Characters are allocated to members of the group, one per player. The characters can be real or fictitious, living or dead. The leader tells each player secretly who their character is, then reads out a list of all the characters. The list is read out twice, slowly, but no player is allowed to take notes. People divide into teams of four or five and sit, in their teams, on chairs. One team is chosen to go first, and they ask any other team if they have any one of the characters from the list (eg 'Do you have Captain Scarlet?'). If Team 2 does, the person whose character it is (eg Captain Scarlet) moves over to Team 1, who then have another turn. If they do not, Team 2 take a turn at doing the asking.

On their first turn at guessing, a team cannot ask for a character who has already been identified. However, if their first guess is successful, they can ask for a character they already know. Players must not reveal their identity to any other person, even the members of their own team. The aim is for players to make their team as large as possible. When around half the characters have been identified, the leader reads the list out again. The game can be adapted to suit younger players by pairing them with an older person and allocating a joint character to them both.

5+ Team Call

People form teams of about eight, and each team is placed in a position equidistant from the leader. He calls out a number of items one by one (eg 'A pair of white socks', 'A silver earring', 'Someone with glasses', 'Someone who is good at spelling', 'A first-class stamp', 'A handbag'). After the leader has specified what it is that he wants, each team has to procure it. When they have done so, someone from the team takes it to the leader. Note that if it is, say, an item of clothing such as a pair of white socks, it must be delivered to the leader off the wearer's feet. The socks can only stay on the wearer's feet if the leader has said, '*Someone wearing* a pair of white socks.' The first team to deliver the required object to the leader's satisfaction wins a point.

5+ Cat, Mouse, Elephant

Play Cruds and Creeps from Session 1, either as a reminder if you have already played it or to learn it. Then this variation may be added. Each line of players decides as a group what animal they are all going to be. They can all be Mice, Cats or Elephants. Each animal has an appropriate action which the leader must demonstrate (eg a curved arm to make a trunk for the Elephant; two hands on either side of the face to make whiskers for the Cat; two hands by the sides of the head to make ears for the Mouse). Each team goes back to their wall to decide on their animals before coming out to face their opponents. The leader counts to three, and the groups make their agreed animal actions. At that point the players work out who chases whom, and the pursuit is under way. The Cats chase the Mice, the Elephants chase the Cats, and the Mice chase the Elephants. If both teams have chosen the same animal, there is no chase.

Trousers

The games in this section continue to foster group cohesion and co-operation as a way of engendering a sense of achievement and satisfaction. Group members should notice a difference in their level of teamwork and communication as a result of time spent together and the things they have been looking at.

3+ One, Two, Clap

The leader creates a rhythm by setting up a simple rule: if he claps once, the group claps back twice; and if he claps twice, the group claps back once. The group will soon get the hang of this, and the leader will establish some very catchy rhythms. He may choose to clap at a pattern or purely at random, but the aim is for the group to enjoy the rhythm they are all creating.

5+ Hand-Tap

People kneel on the floor in a circle, with palms flat on the floor in front of them. The leader sends a tap on the floor around the circle in a clockwise direction. He starts by making a single tap on the floor with his right hand, which is passed to his left hand and then on to the right hand of the person to his left, and so on round the circle. Make sure that the group can send the tap all the way round, so that the speed is fairly constant and a rhythm is set up. Then introduce the idea that if someone taps twice (ie two quavers instead of a crotchet, 'coffee' instead of 'tea'), the tap changes direction. Surprisingly, people sometimes manage to catch themselves out! The game becomes more complex still if the group interlocks arms so that the hand-order is not the same as the person-order. People will forget which hand is theirs!

7+ Buzz

Everyone stands in a circle. Starting with the leader and moving clockwise, they count from one to seven and back down to one again, with each player saying a number in turn ('One, two, three, four, five, six, seven, six, five, four, three, two, one, two, three…'). The count continues until it comes back to the leader again. When this is happening smoothly and naturally, the leader adds to the difficulty by stipulating that this time instead of saying 'Seven', the player whose turn it is says 'Buzz'. When the group has got the hang of this, a further rule is added – instead of saying 'Five' the player says nothing and raises their right foot in the air. (This is now more tricky as players must remember whether the numbers are going up or down.) Add another action for 'Three', and so on, as far as the group is able to take it and still fulfil the task successfully.

7+ This is a Dog

The group forms a circle, and the leader takes two similar but different objects (eg a red pen and a blue pen). He passes one of the objects to the person on his right (**B**), saying 'This is a dog'. In response **B** asks 'A what?' The leader replies 'A dog.' **B** turns to **C** on his/her right and says 'This is a dog.' **C** replies 'A what?' and **B** turns back to the leader and asks 'A what?' The leader says 'A dog', and **B** tells **C** 'A dog' and passes the object to **C**. Each time the question 'A what?' must be passed back round the circle to the leader, and his reply must go forward via each person until it reaches the person who is receiving the object. Once the object has been passed round the entire circle and back to the leader, the group can practise the second part of the game by doing exactly the same thing with the second object; only this time it is passed to the left and the statement becomes 'This is a cat'. Once the second object has gone round the circle, and both are back in the leader's possession, the fun begins! The leader passes the first object to the person on his right, saying 'This is a dog'. Then he immediately passes the second object to the person on the left, saying 'This is a cat'. There may come a point halfway round the circle when the game completely collapses!

THE BOTTLE BANK

Brown

These games are about using diversity rather than trying to overcome it.

Gadgets (3+)

People divide into small groups of three or four, and the leader asks each group to think of an electrical gadget that might be found in a kitchen. The whole group must then become that gadget, making as accurate a representation as they can. They should be encouraged to think about the gadget's shape, its moving parts and the noises it makes. People are allowed five minutes or so to work on this, and then in turn the groups show their gadget to the others. As they do so, they must emphasise the different components in the gadget and how each is necessary for the whole. Look out for groups who have used players' specific attributes to portray different parts of the gadget (eg someone tall bending over to hold the 'blades' of a food mixer).

The chances are that more than one group will have chosen the same gadget. If this is so, the leader should emphasise how each has highlighted different aspects of the same thing.

All-Sorts People (3+)

Each group is given either a large box of Liquorice Allsorts or a pile of plastic/card shapes that includes spares – rectangles, triangles, hexagons, as rich a diversity of shapes as possible. Then they experiment with the sweets or shapes to make as many different people-shapes as possible, perhaps using group members as models. The diversity that can be achieved should be emphasised, and a large mirror be made available so that the groups can look at each other in turn. Diversity is exciting because it means that we are each unique, with our own strengths and abilities. We need each other; everyone has something to offer.

The leader then describes some tasks, asking each group what they could do to help each other achieve their task. Two examples are:

1. The car needs cleaning inside and out. Who washes the hub caps? The roof? The windows? Who clears rubbish from the nooks and crannies inside the car?
2. The cat is stuck up a tree. Who could help to encourage it down? Climb the tree? Fetch the ladder and hold it? Phone the fire brigade? Cuddle the cat once it is down?

Obstacle Races (5+)

This is an obstacle race, with as much variety as possible in the obstacles, eg things to crawl through, to climb over, requiring balance and precision, requiring speed, requiring stamina. Run it as a timed event. People divide into teams of four, and each team runs the race as a relay. Obviously, the fastest team wins. Afterwards, teams discuss the course and note which bits different team members were particularly good at.

Green

These exercises encourage players to think of themselves in context and about the variety of different relationships they have with all sorts of people.

Friendship Map (3+)

All you need for this exercise is paper and pencil and the ability to draw stick figures. In the centre of the page draw yourself and label the figure 'Me'. Then think of your friendships and family relationships, and draw figures to represent these people, putting those with whom you share most deeply closest to 'Me' and those with whom you are on friendly 'nodding terms' furthest away. Other figures will come somewhere between the two extremes. Write the initials of your friends next to the appropriate figures. You have now produced your 'friendship map' showing the network of friendships you have, and where help and support is available to you.

While others are making friendship maps, the youngest members of the group can simply draw pictures of themselves and their friends, without worrying where they are placed in relation to self.

Button Sculpt (5+)

This exercise is like the one in Session 1 (p 17). This time people apply the activity to themselves in their real situations – their family, their class, their workplace. If they want to, they can talk the process through with someone else, but confidentiality must be guaranteed at the beginning of the exercise. However, if members of the same household are present, they may like to share their perceptions so as to increase understanding of each other – but, again, only if they want to do so.

Network (7+)

The group sits in a circle and one person (**A**) is given a ball of wool. **A** chooses someone in the group (**B**) and says 'You are…and you help me by…', stating the kind of relationship **B** has with **A**, including why and how **B** helps **A**, eg 'You are my younger sister and you help me by feeding my gerbil sometimes'. As he/she does this, **A** keeps hold of the end of the wool and throws the ball to **B** who repeats the process with someone else (**C**), keeping hold of the wool at a point that makes it taut with **A**. You may find that you have a situation where **A** says to **B**, who really is **A**'s daughter, 'You are my daughter and you help me by…'! People must be encouraged to think widely and at many different levels. Players can have more than one go, each time holding the wool at a point that makes it taut with the person from whom it was received. The ball is thrown from person to person. By the end a network of wool that is strong and complex will result – an image of the network of support that is available to each player.

Clear

The games in this section are about expressing intimacy, trust and care for one another. Use the Wheely Bins for these.

3+ 'I like You, I like Me'

The group sits on chairs which are arranged in a circle. The leader must impose a strict discipline that nobody evaluates or comments upon anything that anyone else says. In turn, players around the circle must say something they like about themselves. They may need a moment to think. Each person must say it out loud, and the rest of the group must listen. Then, going round the circle again, each person asks for three different people to say something that they like about him/her. This is a difficult (and long) exercise but can be very powerful. Some children under five may well join in this game with some encouragement. They will certainly benefit from affirmative comments and appreciation.

7+ Group Sculpt

This is a little like Thank You (p 25), but the activity is done in silence and with more concentration. Each person thinks of one thing he/she contributes to the whole group. They are given a few moments to think. If they are stuck, they should be encouraged to ask for help rather than other players offer it. Then a volunteer (**A**) walks to the middle of the room and takes up a pose that represents what he/she contributes. The leader then asks for another volunteer (**B**), or chooses someone with a touch on the shoulder. **B** joins **A** and also takes up a representative pose, which doesn't necessarily touch **A**'s. Gradually, people are added one at a time, until everyone is part of the 'sculpture'. After a moment of silence, the sculpture dissolves and the group reads 1 Corinthians 12:12–27 together.

10+ Group Breathe

This is the same as Group Sculpt but people do not take up a pose. Rather, **B** joins **A** and touches him/her in such a way as to feel the rhythm of **A**'s breathing. **B** adjusts his/her own breathing to match. **C** finds the rhythm of **B**'s breathing and joins in, and so on. As above, when everyone is breathing in harmony, the group stops to read 1 Corinthians 12:12–27 together.

CAN RECYCLING CENTRE

Watch Scrap Happy – The Video Part 5.

3+ Treats

Mr. Scrap suggested cream cakes as a treat. What treats do the members of your group give to themselves – a bubble bath, an ice cream, a bunch of flowers? Discuss these together.

3+ Song Time

Members of the group celebrate using the Scrap Happy Song and 'Dem bones' (p 92–94), encouraging movement, dance and the use of percussion instruments. People can also share favourite jokes from *Scrap Happy* and others that they know.

5+ OK News 5

Read this part of the Scrap Happy Story and play the Scrap Family Game (photocopy pp 48–49, one for each group of four players). Those who have seen the video could go straight to the game.

7+ Wordsearch

The 'Piecing It Together' wordsearch (p 66) is photocopied and given to the group who have split into pairs, preferably with children linked to adults. While they do the wordsearch in their pairs, the leader can point out that keeping peace between us takes time, effort and skill. People are encouraged to clarify the meanings of words in the wordsearch. Are there other words or phrases that might have been in the wordsearch if there had been more space (eg 'cherish', 'peacemaker', 'empathise', 'look for good')?

10+ Learning Network 1

In groups of six or eight, or in their Wheely Bins, people reflect on the Scrap Happy Story. Each character is considered in turn. What has each individual learned and from whom? For example, Kitty learned the importance of working together from all the Scrap Family; Nigel learned that Belinda had forgiven him and loved him when Belinda bought his favourite cream cake.

The characters of the Scrap Family, Orlando and Kitty are drawn around the edge of a large sheet of paper, each figure in a different colour so that he/she is easily recognisable. When a piece of learning has been identified, a line is drawn from the learner to the person from whom it was learned (use a pen of the learner's colour). Soon a 'Learning Map' is built up, showing that everyone learns from everyone else.

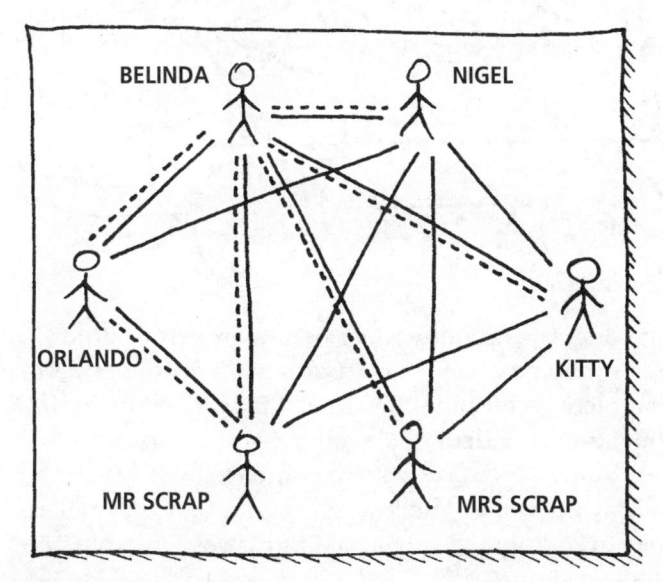

15+ Learning Network 2

The leader asks the groups to go back beyond part 5 of *Scrap Happy – The Video* to earlier episodes. Are there pieces of learning from these that they can discover? The idea of negative learning can be introduced, eg Belinda learned that she was not very important when the rest of the family would not let her wear a red nose. The groups indicate any negative learning on their Learning Maps by drawing dotted lines in the learner's colour. The leader should point out that we all learn from each other. Sometimes this learning can be helpful, and sometimes it isn't. Unhelpful, even damaging learning is usually unintentional – it was in the Scrap Family – so it is important that we keep communicating, forgiving and working at our relationships.

GARDEN WASTE

3+ Favourites

The group are given the choice to repeat one or two favourite games to round off this section.

JUMBLE SALE

3+ Summer Fair

Each Wheely Bin group creates two different stalls or activities. An example is Penny-in-the-Bucket, where a penny is placed in the bottom of a bucket of water. Others try to drop their pennies into the water so that they land on top of the first penny. Wheely Bins should also be responsible for staffing their activities, perhaps by devising a rota so that everyone has an opportunity to visit other stalls. To ensure variety, one person should be given the names of all the suggestions and inform Wheely Bin groups if they need to think of alternatives. The activities, indoors or out, are set up at an agreed time and there should also be an agreed finishing time. In pairs or small groups, everyone should be able to find something that they are good at and can enjoy.

Here are some other suggestions for activities:

1. Apple-Bobbing – apples float in water, and people try to pick them up with their teeth (keeping hands behind the back).
2. Pegs-on-a-Line – a washing line is strung up at child-height and twelve pegs fixed along it. Keeping one hand behind his/her back, each player tries with the other hand to take as many pegs off the line as possible.
3. Lego/Duplo Towers – people build the highest towers they can in one minute. Individuals try to improve their own best score. Pairs or groups could co-operate to build giant towers and practice at improving on their best height.

3+ Design Your Own Pizza

This could be incorporated into the Summer Fair. Provide mini pizza bases, or rounds of thick bread, and a selection of pizza toppings (eg tomato puree, pulped tomatoes, grated cheese, pineapple chunks, fresh tomatoes, mushrooms, ham, sausages). Individuals choose their own toppings, (you may want to limit them to three choices) and design their pizzas. An adult with a catering 'health and hygiene' certificate might oversee this activity, especially the cooking of the pizzas.

3+ Inter-Church Afternoon

Members of another church, perhaps from a different Christian tradition, could be invited to join with your own group for an afternoon or evening event. Ask the church to bring people of all ages. Your programme should encourage interaction between people from the two churches and across the age groups. When planning, your own group members should take time to reflect on the *Scrap Happy* sessions they have already used. What worked for them in helping people to relax and relate across age groups? Some of these could be built into your inter-church programme. Remember to include:

1. Warm-up activities to help people relax.
2. Small-group activities to help people meet in twos, fours, sixes, and across the generations.
3. Opportunities to tell stories about self, home, church and the world, and to share ideas and concerns. Use activities such as an adapted version of the game in **OK News 1**. You will need to change the topics that people talk about to suit your event.
4. Time to enjoy a meal together. The provision of food is always 'a winner', but keep it simple.

When they have planned the event mentally, the planners should step into the shoes of the people they have invited and go through the programme seeing it from their point of view. Will it feel comfortable for those coming, or do you need to adjust your plan?

At the actual event it will be better for folk to form a few, in-depth relationships with guests than to try to get to know everyone. Your programme can be adjusted to use with other churches in the future.

3+ Uniform Picnic

Various households are invited to a bring-and-share picnic or lunch. It will be necessary to plan carefully beforehand what to ask households to bring, and the leader should let them know *privately* what their contribution is. However, he should also tell each household to tell anyone else who asks that they are bringing sausages. The rumour will get around that everyone is bringing sausages! How uninteresting to have all the food the same, when there is such a diversity of food available!

See what happens on the day when the guests arrive and there is a splendid array of food. How many people actually do bring sausages? The group can discuss what happened, and enjoy the diversity of food along with the company of so many different people.

5+ Scrapmobile Drive

This is like a Beetle Drive but, to link in with the Scrap Happy theme, people draw a scrapmobile instead. Enough tables are needed to seat four people per table, in pairs facing each other. Paper, pencils and a dice are on each table, with score sheets that have been prepared beforehand. The tables are placed around the room and numbered in sequence. Pairs play opposite one another for an agreed number of games, each taking the dice in turn. All tables start together. Players throw the dice and draw different parts of the scrapmobile depending on the number they have thrown.

The scores for the different parts of the Scrapmobile are: Engine – 6; Body – 5; Wheel – 4; Steering wheel – 3; Seat – 2; Driver – 1.

The engine and body must be drawn before other parts may be added. The first person on the table to complete a scrapmobile shouts 'Drive!' At this point the game is ended, and each pair totals up their combined score. Scores are compared with the other pair at the table. The lowest-scoring pair stay where they are while the other pair move on one table in a clockwise direction.

SCORES	POSSIBLE	ACTUAL
Engine	6	
Body	5	
Wheels	16 (4 x 4)	
Steering Wheel	3	
Seats	6 (3 x 2)	
Driver	1	

An agreed number of games should be fixed on beforehand. After they have all been played, the leader totals up the scores to find the winning pair and gives them a cheer. The real 'winning' in the game is for everyone, because the process is such good fun.

SWEEPING UP

Red Nose (3+)

Each Wheely Bin group sits in a circle and a plastic red nose is passed around while music is played. When the music stops, the person with the nose wears it and tells the group what, for them, has been the best thing about belonging to the Wheely Bin. Anyone who gets a second turn tells the group what they have enjoyed about Session 5.

Affirmation (3+)

Each person is given a gingerbread-man shape cut out of paper, on which they write their name and draw or write the following:

* things they have valued about this and previous sessions
* anything they hope to do as a result of the session

When they have done this, people can show their gingerbread figures and share what they want to with the rest of the group.

Then the group sits in a circle with the gingerbread figures in front of their owners. Have available piles of blank paper and pencils or felt pens. Each person is invited to think of everyone else in the group and to write or draw appreciative messages for each one, to say 'Thank you' for being part of the group. They also say what special treat they would like to give to the others and why.

Younger children may participate at the level of drawing pictures for everyone and a gingerbread figure for themselves. They will appreciate receiving pictures and messages themselves. The 'givers' will need to explain their messages. These are placed on the appropriate gingerbread figure so that each person receives a pile of messages to take home.

Sing and Pray (3+)

The group prays together and sings the Scrap Happy Song and perhaps 'He's got the whole world in his hands'.

*Lord and heavenly Father,
through your Son Jesus Christ
you have called us to be one,
in (our homes and in) the family of your Church:
give us grace to break down the barriers
which keep us apart;
that accepting our differences,
we may grow in love for one another,
to the glory of your name.*

(A prayer from Northern Ireland, quoted in PRAYERS FOR EVERYONE, Frank Colquhoun, Triangle. Words in brackets have been added)

Human Letters (3+)

Just for fun, this section could end with a game that is a variation of Body Letters (p 13). Using their bodies like vertical letters, members of the group spell each other's names in turn, then the words 'Scrap Happy' and any other significant words that have arisen during this session or series of sessions.

Reflection (7+)

The group takes time to reflect on the session. What were the high points (best things) and low points (worst things) for each person? With whom have they shared and developed relationships today? What have they learned about arguments and making up quarrels?

Guided Thoughts (15+)

With some music playing quietly in the background, people are invited to think about their own relationships. The leader should guide them as follows:

1. Bring to your mind your family or closest friends, each person in turn. As you think of them, remember how they have enriched your life... What have they shared with you and given you?
2. Think of yourself... What have you brought to their lives?
3. Think further about these relationships... Are any of them vulnerable? Are there any unresolved differences or misunderstandings, things left unsaid? What maintenance does each relationship need?
4. What would you like to say to each person?
5. What would you like to do with each person?

*Lord, we bring to you ourselves and those close to us.
Thank you for them.
Please help us to nurture and maintain these relationships
even when it is hard and takes courage.
Help us to keep communicating,
to keep loving and forgiving each other.
May our families be communities of love
in which all are valued and can journey well together.*

NB Leaders need to think ahead and check with participants before taking them through the reflection. **OK Info 3** contains one idea for developing all-age groups that support all types of household.

Piecing it together

This is a wordsearch about making and keeping peace between people. Find the listed words: these may go across, down, backwards or diagonally in the grid. (Answers on page 94.)

```
E D L O V E W K N A H T E
R K I N D N E S S K L A T
U O S V V P L H G U A L A
P A T I E N C E U E R A C
W W E F O R G I V E J K I
X A N A M E S H L E A R N
N C V A L U E I N A H T U
E C N A R E L O T I K N M
G E Y H O N E S T Y E E M
O P E R U T R U N C C R O
T T N O R F N O C D I E C
I A M Z E L T N E G T F E
A N A F A M I L Y G S F T
T C E B M R I F F A U I A
E E T A R E P O O C J D L
D O G O F M O D G N I K E
X C O M M U N I T Y R S R
```

Acceptance   Affirm   Care   Communicate   Community   Confront   Co-operate   Different   Diversity
Family   Forgive   Gentle   Honesty   Justice   Kingdom of God   Laugh   Learn   Listen   Love   Kindness
Names   Negotiate   Nurture   Patience   Relate   Talk   Team   Thank   Tolerance   Value

Being friends, making and keeping peace between us, takes time, effort and skill. We are all human, and sometimes we give and receive unhelpful, even wrong, signals. Quarrels, arguments and soured relationships easily arise if we do not keep communicating and forgiving each other. It takes commitment and practice to keep nourishing our friendships.

© Copyright Scripture Union 1996. May be photocopied by the church or organisation that has bought this book.

OK NEWS

Hello! I'm Orlando. I'm the messy one who likes jokes.

And I'm his sister Kitty. I'm the tidy one.

Orlando: Kitty and I live in a really exciting place. It's the OK Scrapyard. We use other people's scrap – it's very useful stuff and worth a lot. At the moment we're building a Scrapmobile, which is fantastic! The annoying thing is we can't finish it until we find a 'self-tapping, reinforced iron-alloy sprocket with a quarter-inch diam and a flanged cross-head attachment'. It's a tiny, special screw – the Scrapmobile won't work without it. Have you seen one?

Kitty: The Scrap Family Theatre Company are visiting us today. They are going to perform a play for Orlando and me. We might ask them to travel with us in the Scrapmobile. Then other people can see their play. I'm enjoying getting to know Mr and Mrs Scrap and their children, Nigel and Belinda. Mind you, they do seem to have their problems – all because they don't really listen to each other. They have each confided in me secretly.

© Copyright Scripture Union 1996. May be photocopied by the church or organisation that has bought this book.

None of them understands me or really hears what I'm saying.

Nigel doesn't understand me. He doesn't hear what I say half the time.

Belinda doesn't understand me. She doesn't hear what I'm saying.

Father doesn't understand me. He doesn't hear what I'm saying.

Kitty: I didn't know what to suggest. So I said to Orlando, 'I've got this friend who knows this family. Now none of this family seem to understand or listen to each other. They've all complained…to my friend…and none of them know that she knows that each of them has complained to her. What should she do?'

Orlando: Kitty's friend has a tricky situation. I was just thinking about it when I met Mr Scrap – wise chap – and so I asked him what Kitty's friend should do.

Tell your friend to tell the family to all sit down and have a nice cup of tea together and LISTEN to each other.

Mr Scrap has the answer to his own family's problem!

Something to do together

It's good to talk, and it's good to listen. Most families and groups can benefit from listening to each other. Here is a game to encourage you. All you need is a dice. Take turns to throw it. When you throw a number, you must talk for up to one minute about the subject with that number. If you don't like the subject, you can take the Joker.

Topics to talk about

1. Your favourite family/group activity
2. The Scrap Family – what might they say to each other? Why?
3. The game/activity that you have enjoyed most at *Scrap Happy*
4. A time when someone listened to you when you wanted them to
5. How you feel when no one listens to you
6. Something you would like to say to your family or group

   Joker Choose another number

© Copyright Scripture Union 1996. May be photocopied by the church or organisation that has bought this book.

OK NEWS

2

Hello! I'm Orlando.

And I'm Kitty.

We're brother and sister, and we live in the OK Scrapyard.

Kitty: I'm so excited! The Scrap Happy Theatre Company is visiting the Scrapyard. They are wonderful actors – I know because I saw their play. It's brilliant! I wish Orlando had seen it but … he didn't. He must have forgotten the time or something. Mr Scrap said they'll do it again for Orlando. The play is called 'The Story of Luke'. Here it is. Why don't you share out the roles and read the story together.

THE STORY OF LUKE

NB The play is stylised and exaggerated in both movement and speech. Belinda has a non-speaking role.

MR SCRAP:	The Scrap Family presents…
MR & MRS SCRAP *(together):*	…The Story of…
NIGEL *(steps forward):*	…Luke!
MR SCRAP:	Luke had a father.
MRS SCRAP:	Luke had a brother.
NIGEL:	But Luke, he only loved himself…
MR & MRS SCRAP:	…and hated all the others.
MR SCRAP:	Here's the family…
MRS SCRAP:	…Luke, his dad and me…
NIGEL:	…sitting round the dinner table…
ALL:	…gobbling up their tea.
NIGEL:	Slurp!
MR SCRAP:	Gobble!
NIGEL:	Slurp!
MR SCRAP:	Gobble!
NIGEL:	Slurp!
MR SCRAP:	Gobble!
NIGEL:	Burp!

© Copyright Scripture Union 1996. May be photocopied by the church or organisation that has bought this book.

MRS SCRAP *(smacking them both)*:	Mind your manners!
MR SCRAP & NIGEL:	Ow!
BELINDA:	Dring dring!
MR SCRAP:	There's the phone.
BELINDA:	Dring dring!
MR SCRAP *(mimes picking up the phone)*:	Great Uncle Kevin has died at ninety-seven. He's left us all his money, and it adds up to eleven.
NIGEL & MRS SCRAP:	Eleven what?
MR SCRAP:	Thousand!
NIGEL & MRS SCRAP:	Thousand?
MR SCRAP:	Each!
ALL:	OOOOH!
MR SCRAP:	Luke said…
NIGEL:	Look, I want me money now!
MR SCRAP:	So he bought himself a motorbike…
MRS SCRAP:	…and waved goodbye.
NIGEL:	Ciao!
MRS SCRAP:	Luke was far from home.
MR SCRAP:	Luke was all alone.
NIGEL:	But I've got lots of lovely money, so I'll spend it on my own! Screech!

NIGEL:	Now what shall I buy? I know! Table tennis! Snooker!
MR SCRAP:	Ping!
MRS SCRAP:	Pong!
MR SCRAP:	Ping!
MRS SCRAP:	Pong!
MR SCRAP:	Hit!
MRS SCRAP:	Click!
MR SCRAP:	Plop!
NIGEL:	Amusement arcade! Yeah!
BELINDA:	Cachink!
ALL:	Brrrr click!
NIGEL:	Nudge, nudge, nudge!
ALL:	Tingalingaling! Kkshh…
NIGEL:	Jackpot!
MR SCRAP:	Luke was lucky. Life was sunny…
MRS SCRAP:	So he didn't think it funny…
MR & MRS SCRAP *(arm round each other's shoulders, cheesy smiles on faces)*:	…that suddenly he had lots of friends…
MRS SCRAP:	…to help him spend his money!

© Copyright Scripture Union 1996. May be photocopied by the church or organisation that has bought this book.

NIGEL:	Horse racing!
MR & MRS SCRAP:	You bet!
NIGEL:	A thousand pounds on Dead Cert.
MR & MRS SCRAP:	They're off!

(Nigel, Mr & Mrs Scrap mimic following horse's progress with reactions as it takes the jumps – 'Whee!')

BELINDA:	Giddygum, giddygum, giddygum, whee! Giddygum, giddygum, giddygum, whee! Giddygum, giddygum, giddygum…
NIGEL, MR & MRS SCRAP:	Splat!
MR & MRS SCRAP:	Oh dear.
NIGEL:	Ten losers in a row!
MR & MRS SCRAP:	Is there any more money?
NIGEL:	No!
MR & MRS SCRAP:	Time to go.
NIGEL:	Oh!
MRS SCRAP (pushing Nigel who is caught by Mr S):	Cheerio!
MR SCRAP (pushing Nigel upright):	Cheerio!
NIGEL (turning to audience):	Cheerio!

(Nigel continues to fall and is caught by Belinda who lets him fall gently to the floor.)

NIGEL:	Oh!
MR & MRS SCRAP:	Luke, he was so sad.
NIGEL:	Luke had been so bad.
MR & MRS SCRAP:	He thought he was the worst-est son a father ever had.
NIGEL:	All I can do is grovel and go back home to Dad.

(Nigel goes down on his hands and knees and mimes crawling.)

NIGEL:	Grovel, grovel, grovel, grovel.
MR SCRAP:	Meanwhile back at home…
MRS SCRAP:	…my father said to me…
MR SCRAP:	Oh, where can my son be?
MRS SCRAP:	Here I am!
MR SCRAP:	No, the other one.
MRS SCRAP:	He saw him grovelling up the road and shouted out…
MR SCRAP:	Whoopee!
NIGEL:	Dad!
MR SCRAP:	Luke!
NIGEL:	Brother!
MRS SCRAP (glumly):	Luke.
MR SCRAP:	Son!
MRS SCRAP & NIGEL:	Yes?
MR SCRAP (to Mrs Scrap):	No, the other one.

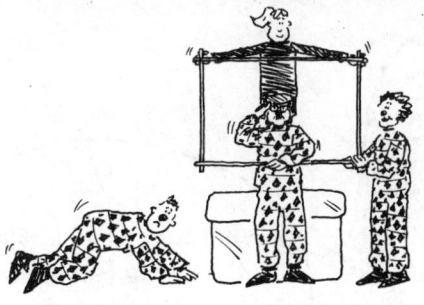

(Mr Scrap goes to Nigel and hugs him.)

MR SCRAP:	Luke, now that you're home, I'm going to…
MRS SCRAP:	…tell him off?
MR SCRAP:	No.
MRS SCRAP:	Stop his pocket money?
MR SCRAP:	No.
MRS SCRAP:	Give him a good hiding?
MR SCRAP:	No! I'm going to have the biggest party ever!
MRS SCRAP:	But he wasted all his money.
MR SCRAP:	But listen! Don't you see? My son's come home to me. Now we can live together, one big happy family.
ALL:	Yeah!
BELINDA (making trumpet fanfare sound):	Tarantara!
MR SCRAP:	The End!

(They all bow, Nigel taking far too many.)

© Copyright Scripture Union 1996. May be photocopied by the church or organisation that has bought this book.

> What was so good about the Scrap Family was that they worked together. They made the story come alive.

Now you try forming the motor bike, the slot machine, the racegoers. It's tricky. I admire the Scrap Family – they're a real team.

What did you think of Luke in the play? I hope he learned from all those silly mistakes he made. It's a good thing that he has such a great Dad!

> I was in the dog-house - I missed the play but the Scrap Family did it again, just for me.

Orlando: Wow! It wasn't what I expected but was…well….profound. You see, Belinda was missing. Apparently she and Nigel squabbled, and the whole family seemed to be out of sorts with one another – scrappy! Anyway, the family put on the play without Belinda…and it was a disaster. They thought they could manage without her, but they couldn't. Her role in the play is important. They need her. Funny really… Kitty said the Scrap Family worked so well together. They might do that when they are together performing, but behind the scenes it's another story. I suppose they're like lots of families.

What's Missing? Who's Missing?

© Copyright Scripture Union 1996. May be photocopied by the church or organisation that has bought this book.

OK NEWS

3

Hello! It's me again – Orlando.

And I'm here too – Kitty.

We're perplexed! No one knows where Belinda is.

Orlando: The Scrap Family performed their play for me. It was disastrous – but very funny. So much went wrong because Belinda was missing. She may not have a speaking part or a red nose, but the play doesn't work without her.

Kitty: I was embarrassed when Orlando saw the Scrap Family doing 'The Story of Luke'. You see, I'd told him they were brilliant. But without Belinda they were awful. It is awful without Belinda. She's been away for a while, so we're all going to plan our search for her.

Have you ever lost someone or something and had to hunt for them? How did you feel?

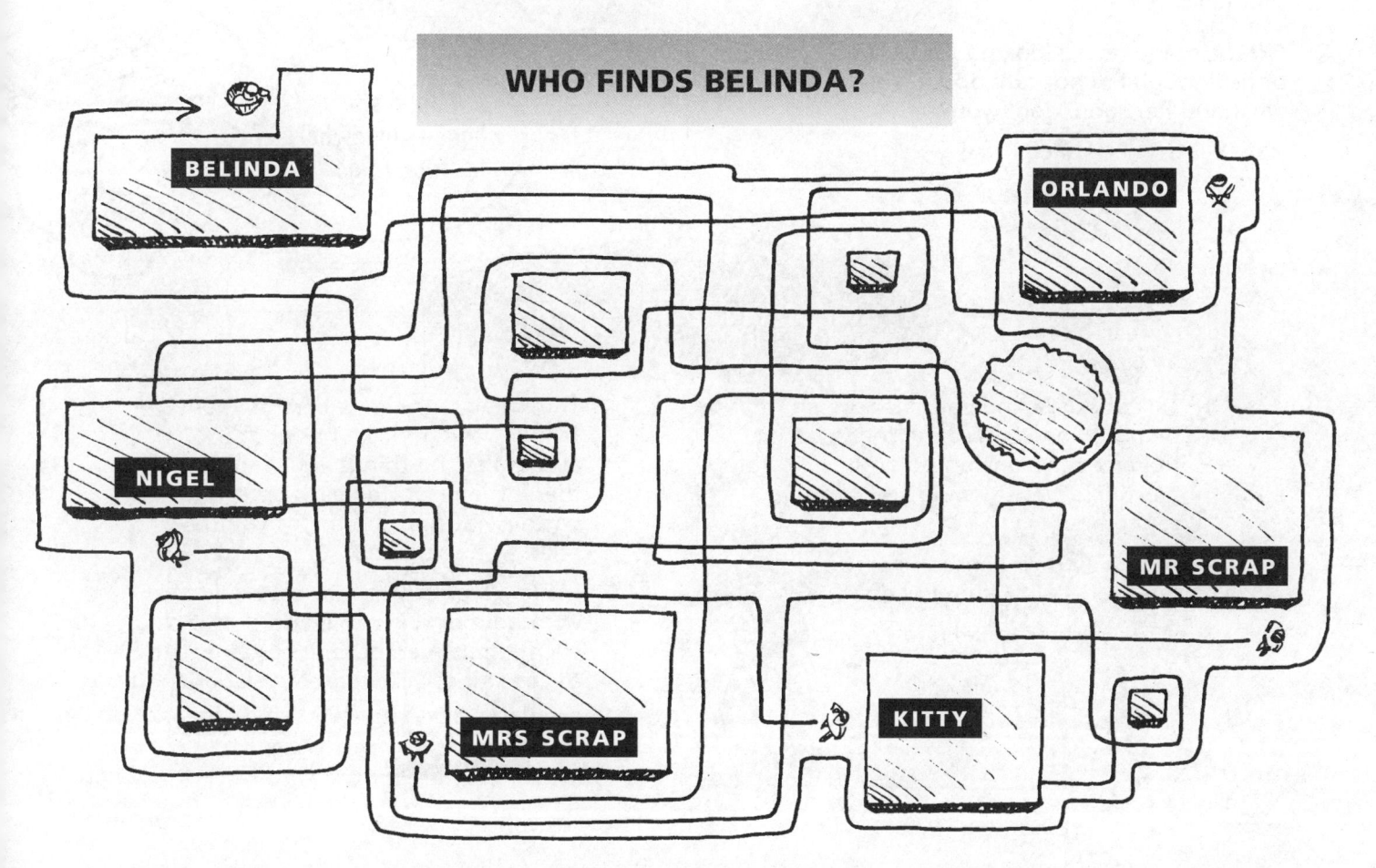

WHO FINDS BELINDA?

BELINDA

ORLANDO

NIGEL

MR SCRAP

MRS SCRAP

KITTY

© Copyright Scripture Union 1996. May be photocopied by the church or organisation that has bought this book.

I've run away from home but it's horrible.

Oh Lord, keep the little love safe wherever she is.

Whatever I do, Nigel and Belinda end up arguing.

Orlando and I don't always see eye to eye.

I'm glad Belinda's out of the way.

I hope she's chosen somewhere nice to go

Belinda: You can't do much with a toothbrush – and that's all I've got. But I'm not going back – they're all horrible to me. They never listen, I get the blame, and I'm too unimportant to have a speaking part in the play. One day I'll be a somebody. Oh, what should I do?

Orlando: We're still looking for Belinda – all of us, though I'm not sure about Nigel. I think we'll find her soon, don't you?

Something to do together

1. Talk about Belinda and her dream of being 'a somebody'. She feels unimportant, unwanted and worthless. What would you like to say to her?

2. How would you answer her question, 'What should I do?'

3. Write a letter to Belinda.

4. Think about the members of your family – the good things about them, and the things you want to thank them for. Tell each person (or write a note) of the things you have been thinking about.

5. Make a star out of card covered with gold or silver foil, and give it to each family member as you tell them of the things you appreciate about them? They are all stars!

© Copyright Scripture Union 1996. May be photocopied by the church or organisation that has bought this book.

OK NEWS

4

Hello! Orlando here!

And Kitty here!

Belinda's back!

Kitty: I found her in a dustbin, of all places. There was a noise near the bins. I thought it was one of my cats, but it was Belinda sobbing…in a dustbin. Fancy running away to a dustbin! At first Belinda said she was not coming home – nobody wanted her, nobody loved her and the Scraps could do the play without her. As you know, that's rubbish. I told her, 'The play was dreadful without you.'

© Copyright Scripture Union 1996. May be photocopied by the church or organisation that has bought this book.

Kitty: Belinda still wasn't convinced, so I found an old clock. We looked at the different parts. I asked, 'Which bits are the most important?' She thought, and then the penny dropped. Every bit is important. Every bit is needed.

But then Belinda said something *very* important: 'I suppose you could say that the clock needed someone to oil the parts and keep it working…' So I said, 'Belinda, that's brilliant! Everyone's important, and without love things go wrong.' And I told her about how much God loves her.

Anyway she came home, said she was sorry and the family were so relieved – except Nigel. I'm not sure about him.

Orlando: Nigel's struggling. He finds it hard having a sister. They are like lots of sisters and brothers – always arguing. Kitty and I argue.

I had a good chat with Nigel about films. He likes Indiana Jones movies. I like *African Queen*. We have different tastes in films. Anyway, the chat helped a bit. Nigel said his sister drives him mad, but I think I helped him to see that life is messy and it is all part of our journey. Indiana Jones' journeys are usually risky and adventurous. Sometimes our life journeys can be like that – full of risk and adventure. But they can also be very messy.

> Kitty told me, "God's love never runs out."

> Orlando told me, "God is always with us."

> Life is messy. We couldn't sleep last night. Orlando and Kitty were having a noisy argument. They're like another brother and sister we know!

Something to do together

1 Kitty and Orlando are angry with each other. Have you any tips for them? What might they do to be friends again?

2 Think of your own life-journey. Draw some pictures, or write a paragraph, about four different events in your life-journey. When have you been aware of the messiness of your life?

3 Show others what you have drawn or written, and share some of your life story.

© Copyright Scripture Union 1996. May be photocopied by the church or organisation that has bought this book.

OK NEWS

Orlando here! Sometimes Kitty really annoys me. But I still love her.

Kitty here! Orlando makes me angry. But I still love him.

We agree on some things, though. Read on...

Kitty: Have you ever been so angry with someone that you nearly exploded? I was like that with Orlando. He is so messy. As fast as I tidy up, he makes everything untidy. Then there's the Scrapmobile. We couldn't decide how to use it. I wanted to do one thing. He wanted to do another. So he started to scrap the Scrapmobile, and I took the pieces back out of the bins. It's in pieces and needs to be fitted together again. I was so angry I could not speak to Orlando.

Orlando: I was really annoyed with Kitty. Didn't speak to her. It was the Scrap Family who helped us to see how stupid we were being. We needed to listen to some of the words of advice we had given them in the past. You know – listen, talk, try to understand, remember God is with you, all that stuff. They were happy today because Belinda is back. Everyone was apologising to everyone else. Even Nigel told Belinda he was sorry. They were talking, trying to understand, forgiving one another and working together. They performed their play. It was brilliant, even better than the first time Kitty saw it. This time Belinda had a red nose, and the Scrap family were not pretending any more. They were working together well on stage and off it. After that, Kitty and I had to agree.

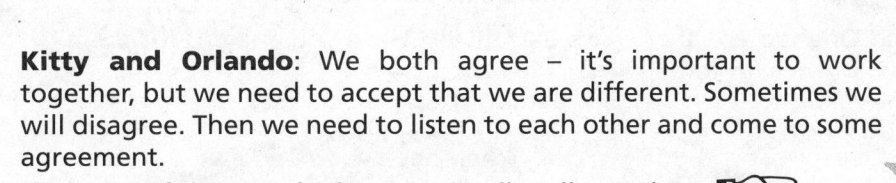

Kitty and Orlando: We both agree – it's important to work together, but we need to accept that we are different. Sometimes we will disagree. Then we need to listen to each other and come to some agreement.

The story of the two donkeys says it all. Pull together! 👉

© Copyright Scripture Union 1996. May be photocopied by the church or organisation that has bought this book.

Peaceful Problem Solving

Published by Quaker Peace & Service. Used with permission.

And we agree that God is with us, and he will help us to face our differences – there's no need to run away.

Now why not play the Scrap Family Game together? It's on pages 48 and 49.

© Copyright Scripture Union 1996. May be photocopied by the church or organisation that has bought this book.

Scrap Art Info 1

Collecting Rubbish

The amount of rubbish we throw away is increasing. Did you know that each year the average household throws away 600 cans, two trees' worth of paper, as well as piles of plastic, rags and glass? What a waste! Much can be reused or recycled.

Re-using: The golden rule is: make sure it is clean.

Recycling: Sort your rubbish. Much of it can be taken to the recycling bins usually found outside your local supermarket. Recycling reduces pollution, saves resources and energy. It creates jobs for people too.

Re-using and recycling are ways of responding to God's call on us to care for the earth.

COLLECT

Different papers: newsprint, computer print-outs, magazines, old rolls of wallpaper, sweet wrappings

Card: birthday and Christmas cards, corrugated card, box card (eg from cereal packets), big and small cardboard boxes

Glass: jars, bottles, different shapes and colours

Metal: wire coat hangers, foil containers, cans (be careful of sharp edges), chicken wire, wire and piping, magnets

Plastic: bottles, containers, bags, tubes, washing-up liquid containers

Rags: old T-shirts, dresses, skirts, shirts, bedding sheets, pillowcases, socks, cardigans

Miscellaneous: sponges, old dish-mops, toothbrushes, nail brushes, balls of wool, cotton, buttons

STORE

Sort the rubbish. Once you are sure it is clean (eg cans are washed out), store it in skips.

Skips can be made from large cardboard boxes, decorated and painted (eg cover with lining paper and hand-print your decoration). Ensure that the corners are smooth and strengthened by covering them with wide, strong adhesive tape. Label the outside of each skip so that everyone knows what is to be kept in it.

Note: you may decide that some types of rubbish are unsuitable for use with your groups (eg glass). Collect them nevertheless. They can go to the recycling bins when you have completed Session 5, along with other junk which you don't want. It can be used elsewhere. To throw it away is to throw away money. For instance, £65 million pounds' worth of rags are thrown away in Britain every year!

USEFUL ADDRESSES

- Oxfam Wastesaver, Units 5–6, Ringway Industrial Centre, Beck Road, Huddersfield.
- Friends of the Earth, 26–28 Underwood Street, London, N1 7JQ.
- Textile Reclamation Association, 16 High Street, Brampton, Huntingdon, PE18 8TU.
- The Pulp and Paper Information Centre, Papermakers House, Rivenhall Road, Westlea, Swindon, SN5 7BE.

© Copyright Scripture Union 1996. May be photocopied by the church or organisation that has bought this book.

Scrap Art Info 2

Some Ideas For Using Scrap (1)

PAINTING

Use sponges for covering big areas and for printing.

Pieces of sponge in clip pegs will work for smaller areas.

Use toothbrushes to get different effects.

Dish-mops are fun to paint with too.

Spray water-based paint from water-spray containers.

Thicken paint by adding washing up liquid or school glue.

Newspaper can be used to protect surfaces but also to give interesting effects on collage pictures when the print is used at different angles.

Beads, buttons, lace and sequins are also useful.

Metal, eg the insides of mechanical clocks, make interesting pictures when arranged on paper.

COLLAGE AND MONTAGE

Use coloured paper from old magazines, torn into small pieces.

Use letters from banner headlines.

Coloured sweet wrappers that have been 'scrunched up' give interesting and colourful textures.

Try natural objects, eg eggshells, woodshavings, sawdust, shells, pressed autumn leaves, raffia, wool.

Fabrics with different textures can be cut into various shapes and sizes.

WARNING

Do not use small round objects such as beads if children under seven are in the group.

© Copyright Scripture Union 1996. May be photocopied by the church or organisation that has bought this book.

JUNK MODELLING

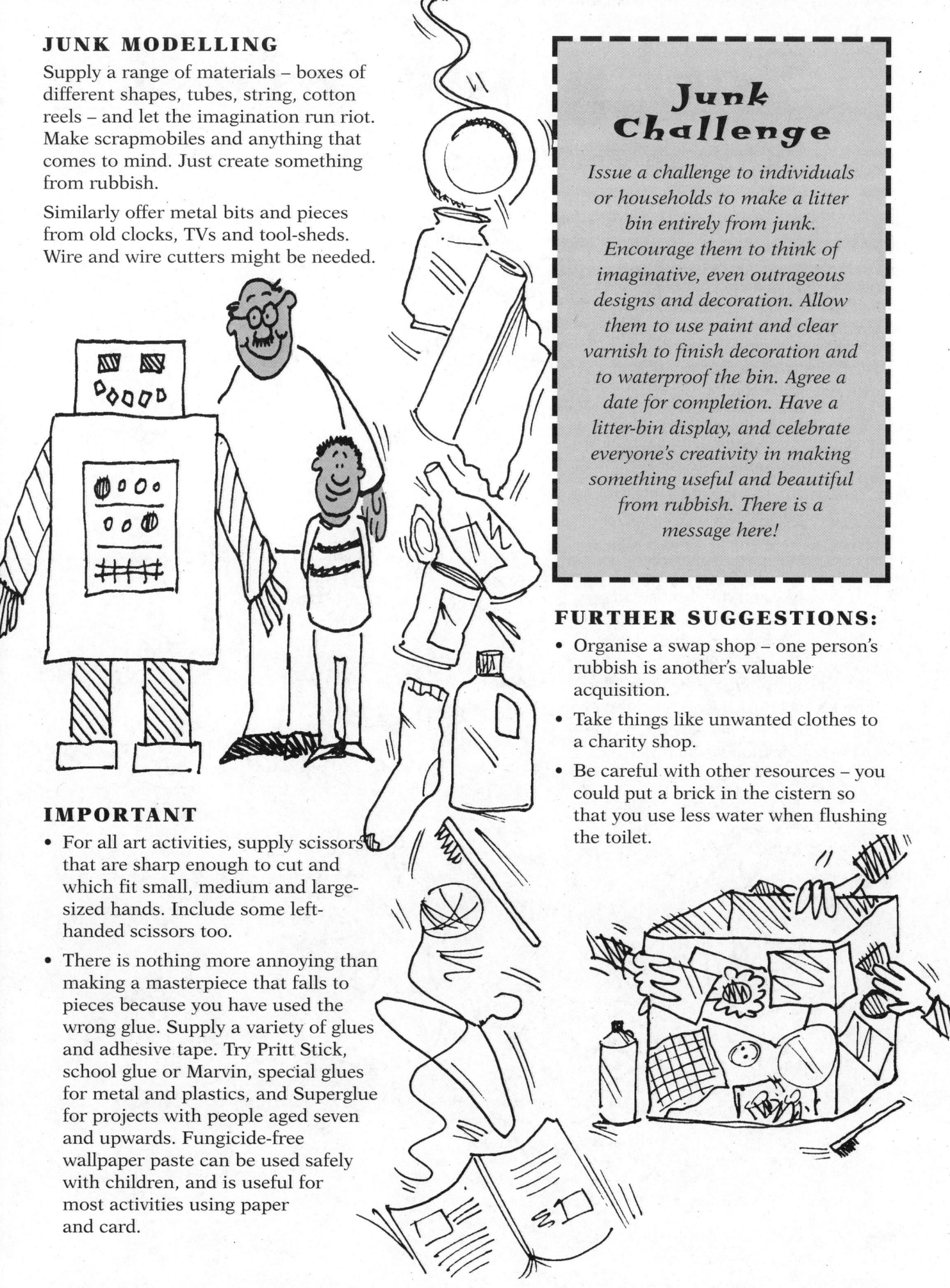

Supply a range of materials – boxes of different shapes, tubes, string, cotton reels – and let the imagination run riot. Make scrapmobiles and anything that comes to mind. Just create something from rubbish.

Similarly offer metal bits and pieces from old clocks, TVs and tool-sheds. Wire and wire cutters might be needed.

IMPORTANT

- For all art activities, supply scissors that are sharp enough to cut and which fit small, medium and large-sized hands. Include some left-handed scissors too.
- There is nothing more annoying than making a masterpiece that falls to pieces because you have used the wrong glue. Supply a variety of glues and adhesive tape. Try Pritt Stick, school glue or Marvin, special glues for metal and plastics, and Superglue for projects with people aged seven and upwards. Fungicide-free wallpaper paste can be used safely with children, and is useful for most activities using paper and card.

Junk Challenge

Issue a challenge to individuals or households to make a litter bin entirely from junk. Encourage them to think of imaginative, even outrageous designs and decoration. Allow them to use paint and clear varnish to finish decoration and to waterproof the bin. Agree a date for completion. Have a litter-bin display, and celebrate everyone's creativity in making something useful and beautiful from rubbish. There is a message here!

FURTHER SUGGESTIONS:

- Organise a swap shop – one person's rubbish is another's valuable acquisition.
- Take things like unwanted clothes to a charity shop.
- Be careful with other resources – you could put a brick in the cistern so that you use less water when flushing the toilet.

© Copyright Scripture Union 1996. May be photocopied by the church or organisation that has bought this book.

Scrap Art Info 3

Some Ideas For Using Scrap: Masks (2)

IDEA 1

You need: old wire coat-hangers; old tights; wool, tissue or fabric for hair; fabric for eyes, nose, mouth; scissors; adhesive.

1. Pull the coat-hanger into the shape you want for the face.

2. Pull a length of the tights material over the coat-hanger, and tie it at the top and the bottom to form the face.

3. Paste wool, tissue paper or fabric on the head for hair.

4. Paste card or fabric onto the face to form the facial features.

5. You could put a different set of features on the back of the mask to show the character in a different mood. Then one side of the coat-hanger heads shows the characters' moods when they work well together and co-operate; and the other side shows their moods when they are not working well together.

© Copyright Scripture Union 1996. May be photocopied by the church or organisation that has bought this book.

IDEA 2

You need: scissors, string, a paper hole-puncher, newspaper, paste, paint and brushes.

1. Paste together sheets of newspaper, 4–6 sheets thick. Cut the pasted sheets into squares, oblongs and circles big enough to cover people's faces. Cut holes in them for the eyes, nose and mouth. Punch two holes at each side of the mask for the face. Press onto an inverted plate, or similar surface, to dry.

2. When the mask is dry, thread a piece of string through the holes on either side of the face, and knot. These will form loops to go over the ears of the person wearing the mask.

3. Build up the features on the face, using small crumpled balls of paper held in place by newspaper strips soaked in paste. Eyebrows, cheeks and the bridge of the nose can be built up in this way.

4. Cover the mask with thin white paper (eg tissue paper) having covered the mask with paste. Push the tissue through the eye holes, mouth, etc, so that they remain.

5. When the mask is dry, paint and add extra features (eg fringed brown paper for hair, a collage hat made from sweet wrappers).

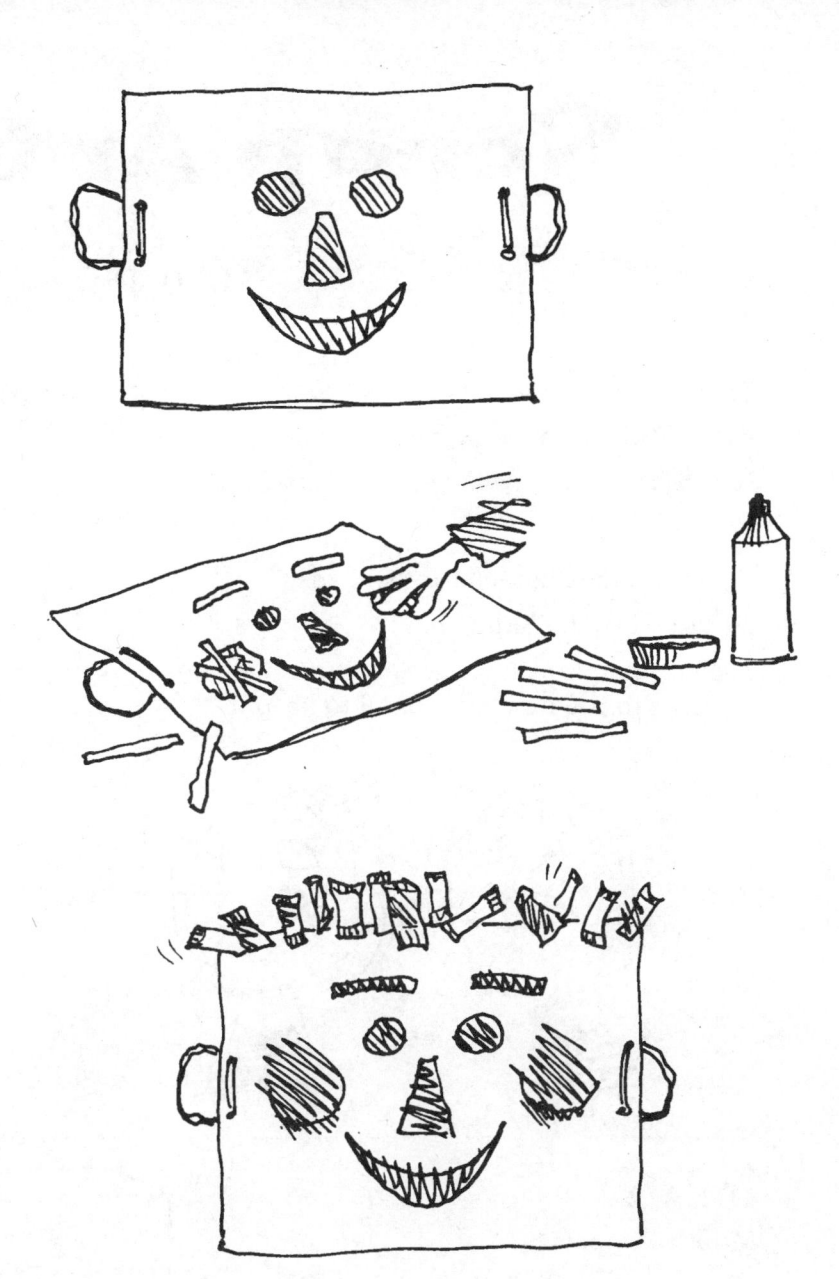

IDEA 3

You need: cardboard plates or card cut into circles, a paper hole-puncher, shearing elastic, felt pens, foil or pipe cleaners, adhesive, scissors.

1. Cut card into circles to cover face.
2. Cut out (cat-shaped) eyes and nose.
3. Pierce holes at each side of the face.
4. Cut cat ears from card, and colour them.
5. Colour the face to represent a Scrap Cat.
6. Attach ears with paste.
7. Attach whiskers made from lengths of foil twisted into shape, or from pipe cleaners.
8. Thread shearing elastic through the holes at the side of the face and knot it, so that it will go behind the head to hold on the cat mask.

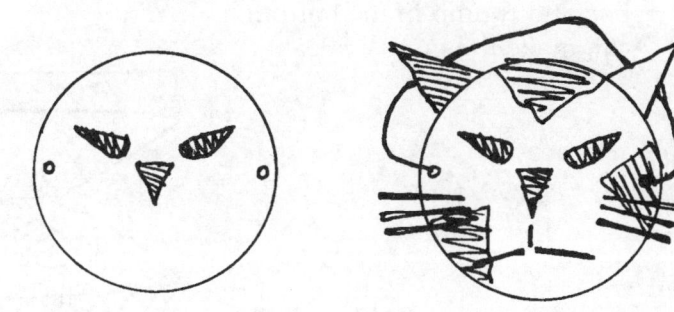

© Copyright Scripture Union 1996. May be photocopied by the church or organisation that has bought this book.

Scrap Art Info 4

Puppets

IDEA 1
Paper-Bag Puppets

You need: plain paper-bags, felt pens, elastic bands.

1. Decide the character to be made.
2. Draw face including hair.
3. Place hand inside bag. Sometimes it helps to use an elastic band to keep it in place.

IDEA 2
Mouth Puppets

You need: paint, small cartons (eg from variety cereal packets), card, scissors.

1. Cut round three sides of a cereal packet.
2. Bend the fourth side to form a hinge.
3. Paint face, mouth, including teeth and inside the mouth.
4. Add card eyes and ears as required.
5. Place four fingers in the top half of the box and thumb in the bottom half. You can make the puppet speak!

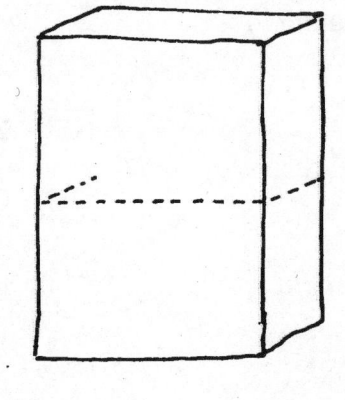

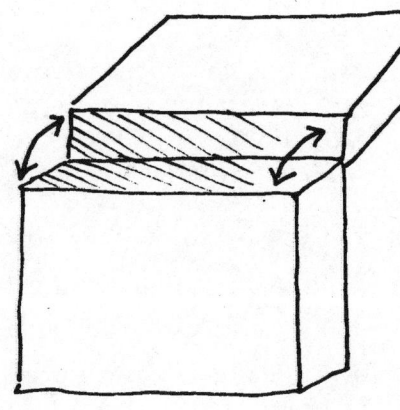

© Copyright Scripture Union 1996. May be photocopied by the church or organisation that has bought this book.

IDEA 3

Cotton Reel/Beads

You need: cotton reels or large threading beads, wool or string, scissors.

1. Knot four lengths of string together, and thread through one cotton reel.
2. Knot string below cotton reel.
3. Separate string keeping two lengths for arms.
4. Thread other two lengths through two cotton reels and knot.
5. Separate threads to form legs. Thread through cotton reels to form feet and knot.
6. Complete arms and knot.

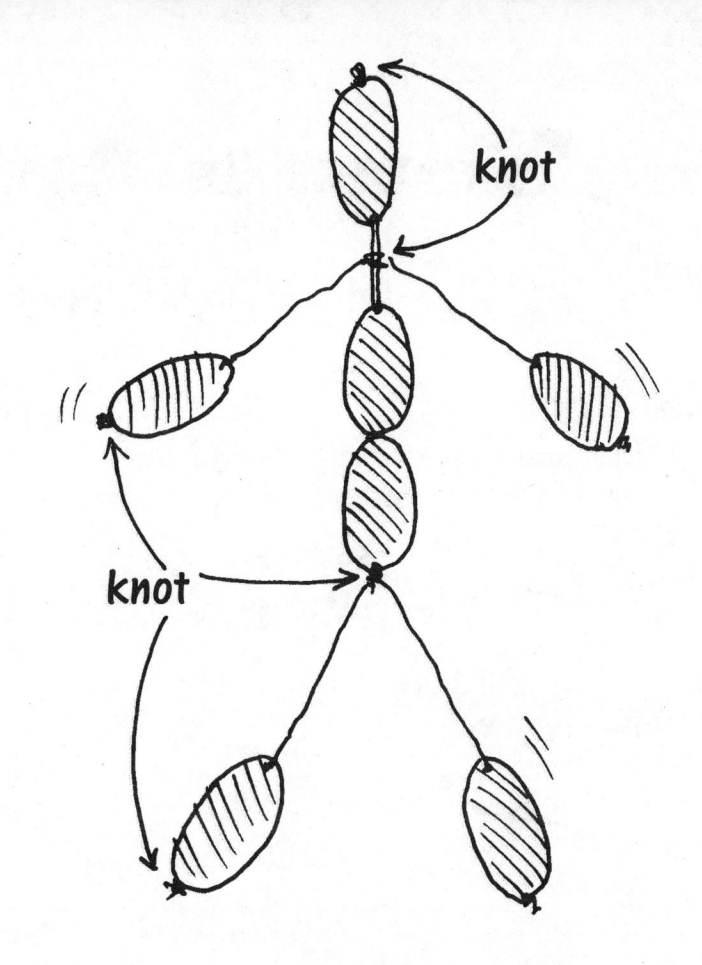

IDEA 4

Glove or Finger Puppets

You need: fabric, scissors, glue, embroidery thread, lace, tape, buttons for decoration, needles and thread. Puppets can be of all sizes.

1. Cut out two identical pieces of fabric in the shape of a Russian doll.
2. Sew the pieces together, leaving the straight edge open for the hand to go in, to work the puppet.
3. Embroider, sew or paste the features on to the face, using fabric, buttons, beads.
4. You may want to paste on hands, belts, buttons.

© Copyright Scripture Union 1996. May be photocopied by the church or organisation that has bought this book.

Scrap Art Info 5

Musical Instruments

SHAKERS

Put dried peas or rice into a container. Seal the lid securely. Decorate the container

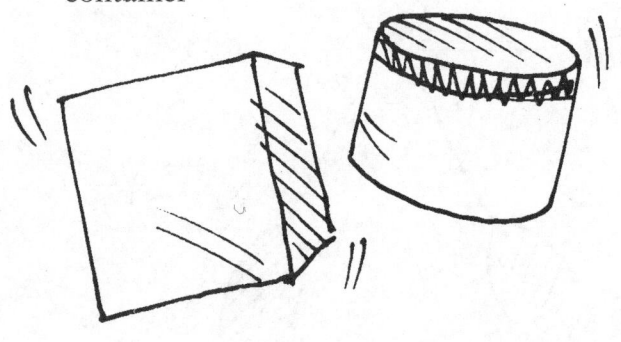

CHIMES

Small kitchen tools or pieces of metal may be hung from a rail to form chimes. Experiment with different tools and metal pieces.

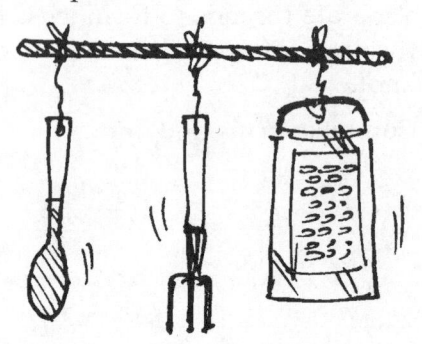

PLASTIC GUITARS

1. Cut a hole in the middle of a plastic bottle (eg near to where the label is).
2. Wedge a piece of broom-handle in the neck of the bottle. Glue in place.
3. Hammer three nails in the far end of the broom-handle, and three tacks towards the bottom of the bottle.
4. Attach lengths of fishing line from the nails to the holes at the bottom of the bottle.
5. Use a small, triangle-shaped piece of wood, or a film container, to place under the strings. Glue in place.

DRUMS

Make a pair of hand drums. Put water or dried beans inside two small tins with plastic lids. (Experiment with various amounts so that you get the sound you want.) Tape the tins together. Use the unsharpened end of a pencil as a drumstick.

Other drums can be made from different-sized tins or cardboard tubes. Stretch strong polythene over the top end of the drum and fix in place with a strong elastic band.

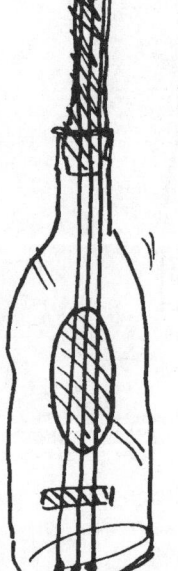

Create your own instruments and sound sculptures. Look at the variety of junk materials available. Design and make your own instruments, eg wind instruments from old kettles. Also make sound sculptures such as wind-chimes. Pipes and tubes are particularly useful. Bottles give melody.

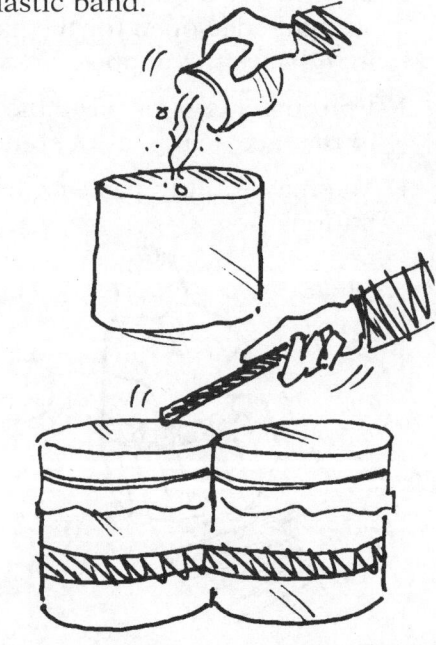

© Copyright Scripture Union 1996. May be photocopied by the church or organisation that has bought this book.

OK Info 1

HOUSEHOLD MEETINGS

Most family or household members lead busy lives. To ensure that time is made to communicate and to nurture home life, why not arrange some household meetings? These can be weekly, fortnightly or monthly – it doesn't matter, so long as they are regular and not easily cancelled or postponed.

Bring everyone together, perhaps at a mealtime, and suggest the idea. Listen to everyone's response. What would be the best day and time for them? Agree a time, a place and a purpose for your first meeting. Agree the tasks to be done, for example who will prepare the food, who will bring paper and pen for setting the agenda, who will plan a particular activity.

PLANNING YOUR AGENDA

Make the agenda available to everyone beforehand, and leave it open so that anyone can contribute.

If there are any, consider children's items first. Include:

- time to share news
- sharing a meal or snacks
- fun items (eg planning the next family outing, deciding holiday destinations)
- a game or time to talk about the news, TV programmes or local events.

Carry items over to the next meeting if the agenda is crowded.

ORGANISING MEETINGS

Schedule meetings regularly and at a convenient time for everybody.

Encourage everyone to speak, and help those with limited vocabulary. Adults should be ready to give children the opportunity to speak first.

Consider all the alternatives when attempting to solve problems or make decisions.

Make clear agreed decisions, and put aside time on future agendas to check that decisions have been carried out.

Reach agreement amongst each other rather than by majority vote. Be prepared sometimes to wait until the next meeting before you make a decision, thus giving people space to think.

Share leadership of meetings so that everyone has the opportunity to learn to lead.

It's football on Thursday.

I have Brownies on Tuesday.

I work late most nights.

I go to my group on Wednesday.

My club's on Friday evening at 8 o'clock.

It looks as if Friday evening would be best for us, say, 6 to 7.45? Does everyone agree?

© Copyright Scripture Union 1996. May be photocopied by the church or organisation that has bought this book.

OK Info 2

Sometimes individuals, families and households need help. Your local Citizens Advice Bureau or council for Voluntary Service will have lists of helping agencies. They can usually point you in the right direction.

ABUSE

- Childline, 2nd Floor, Royal Mail Building, Studd Street, London, N1 0QW; Helpline (0800) 1111.
- National Society for Prevention of Cruelty to Children, 42 Curtain Road, London, EC2A 3NH; Helpline (0800) 800 500.
- Christian Survivors of Sexual Abuse, BM – CSSA, London, WC1N 3XX.
- Safety Net, 14 Virginia Close, New Maldon, KT3 3RB.

ALCOHOL AND DRUGS

- Adfam, 5th Floor, Epworth House, 25 City Road, London, EC1Y 1AA. *(Supports families and friends of drug users.)*
- Alcoholics Anonymous, Box 1, Stonebow House, Stonebow, York, YO1 2NJ. *(See local telephone directory for branch in your area.)*
- Hope UK, 25f Copperfield Street, London, SE1 0EN; tel (0171) 928 0848 (24 hrs).

BEREAVEMENT

- Cruse, Cruse House, 126 Sheen Road, Richmond, Surrey, TW9 1UR; tel (0181) 940 4818.
- Stillbirth & Neonatal Death Society, 28 Portland Place, London, W1N 4DE; tel (0171) 436 5881.

CARERS

- Carers National Association, 20–25 Glasshouse Yard, London, EC1A 4JS; tel (0171) 490 8818.
- Carers Christian Fellowship, 14 Yealand Drive, Ulverston, Lancaster, LA12 8JB; tel (0122) 958 5974.
- Alzheimer's Disease Society, Gordon House, 10 Greencoat Place, London, SW1P 1PH; tel (0171) 306 0606.
- MIND (National Association for Mental Health), Granta House, 15–19 Broadway, London, E15 4BQ; tel (0181) 519 2122.

CHILDREN

- Children's Legal Centre, 20 Compton Terrace, London, N1 2UN; tel (0171) 359 9392.
- Tavistock Clinic, Department of Children & Parents, 120 Belsize Lane, Hampstead, London, NW3 5BA; tel (0171) 435 7111.

COUNSELLING

(For couples together or separately.)

- RELATE, Herbert Gray College, Little Church Street, Rugby, Warks, CV21 3AP; tel (01788) 573241. *(See local telephone directory for branch in your area.)*
- Catholic Marriage Care, Clitherow House, 1 Blythe Mews, Blythe Road, London, W14 0NW; tel (0171) 371 1341. *(See local telephone directory for branch in your area.)*

© Copyright Scripture Union 1996. May be photocopied by the church or organisation that has bought this book.

DEBT

(See local telephone directory for organisations in your area, or contact the Citizens Advice Bureau.)

DEPRESSION & LONELINESS

- The Samaritans (See local telephone directory for branch in your area.)
- MIND *(See above, under CARERS.)*

DISABILITY

- Church Action on Disability, Charisma Cottage, Drewsteignton, Exeter, EX6 6QR; tel (01647) 281259.
- Royal Association for Disability and Rehabilitation, 12 City Forum, 250 City Rd, London, EC1V 8AF; tel (0171) 250 3222.

HIV & AIDS

- The Terence Higgins Trust, 52–54 Gray's Inn Road, London, WC1X 8JU; tel (0171) 831 0330.
- Cara, The Basement, 178 Lancaster Road, London N11 1QU; tel (0171) 792 8299.
- ACET, PO Box 3693, London, SW15 2BQ.

HOUSING/HOMELESSNESS

(Contact local Social Services and housing departments.)

LONE PARENTS

- Gingerbread, 35 Wellington Street, London, WC2E 7BN; tel (0171) 270 0953.
- National Council for One-Parent Families, 255 Kentish Town Road, London, NW5 2LX; tel (0171) 267 1361.
- Broken Rites, 30 Steavenson Street, Bowburn, Durham, DH6 5BA; tel (0191) 377 0205.

MEDIATION AND CONCILIATION

- National Family Mediation, 9 Tavistock Place, London, WC1H 9SN; tel (0171) 383 5993.

OLDER PEOPLE

- Christian Council on Ageing, 20 West Way, Rickmansworth, Herts, WD3 2EN; tel (01923) 774998.
- Age Concern, 1268 London Road, London, SW16 4ER; tel (0181) 679 8000.
- Action on Elder Abuse, 1268 London Road, London, SW16 4ER; tel (0181) 679 8000.
- Grandparents' Federation, Moot House, The Stow, Harlow, Essex, CM20 3AG.

SINGLENESS

- Singularly Significant, Evangelical Alliance, Whitefield House, 186 Kennington Park Road, London, SE11 4BT; tel (0171) 582 6221.

PARENT SUPPORT

- Parentline, Endway House, The Endway, Hadleigh, Essex, SS7 2AN. *(See local telephone directory for branch in your area.)*
- Parent Network, 44–46 Coversham Road, London, NW5 2DS; tel (0171) 485 8535.
- Exploring Parenthood, Latimer Education Centre, 194 Freston Road, London, W10 6TT; tel (0181) 960 1678.
- Family Caring Trust, 44 Rathfriland Rd, Newry, Co. Down, BT34 1LD; tel (01693) 64174.

YOUNG PEOPLE

- National Youth Agency, 17–23 Albion Street, Leicester, LE1 6GD; tel (0116) 285 6789.
- Frontier Youth Trust, 70–74 City Road, London, EC1Y 2BJ; tel (0171) 336 7744. *(They will put you in touch with youth workers who may be able to help.)*

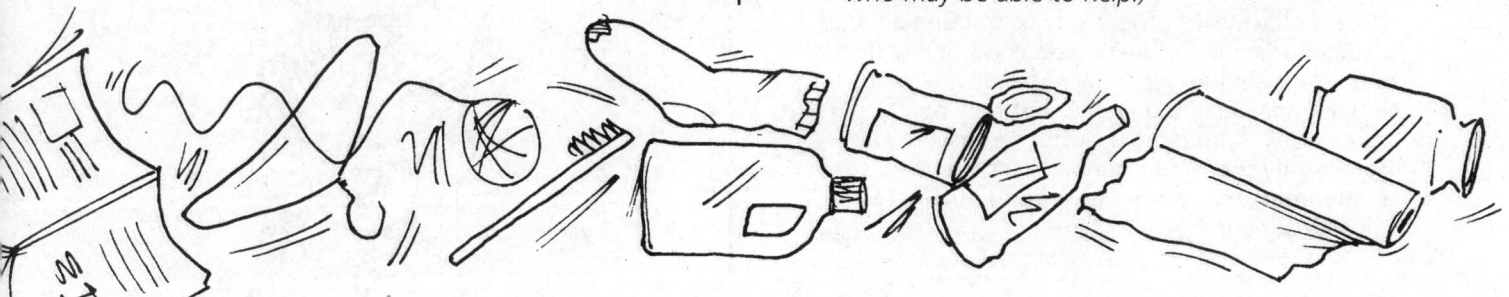

© Copyright Scripture Union 1996. May be photocopied by the church or organisation that has bought this book.

OK Info 3

AFTER SCRAP HAPPY, WHAT NEXT?

HOUSEHOLD CLUSTERS

A household cluster is a group of four or five households who commit themselves to meet regularly for their own mutual benefit. These households can include those who live alone, married and unmarried adults, those with children and those without.

Household clusters offer a way of creating all-age extended family for their members, a family that is local. Modern life, especially urban living, tends to isolate individual households; but they need community. A household cluster can become a community that is small enough for everyone to relate intimately, yet big enough to nurture individual households.

Benefits include:

- Opportunities to build in-depth relationships across the generations; relationships of greater honesty and intimacy in which love, acceptance, freedom, reconciliation and hope are experienced.
- Friendships and companionship with those one would not normally meet.
- The childless have contact with children.
- Children form friendships with other significant adults and with other children.
- People discover how families other than their own function.
- Social and practical support develops for individuals and households.
- Lots of fun together.

Clusters need:

- Commitment from each household, perhaps an agreement among them to meet initially every fortnight for the first three or four months.
- A regular meeting time that takes into account the needs of children, the elderly and people's working lives. Early evening on a Friday or Saturday might be popular, or Sunday afternoons (often a difficult time for those who live alone).
- A place to meet. Homes are popular so give people the opportunity to use their homes. Foster hospitality, but recognise that some homes may be too small for the group.
- Leaders who work as a pair and who can facilitate the sessions to ensure that they are planned and enabled by others. After a while some clusters may pass the planning around to households, or a couple of households, but retain their leaders. It is exciting to hear how creative children can be in such planning sessions.
- Agreed expectations and goals. From time to time these will need re-negotiating, and require honest but sensitive discussion.

© Copyright Scripture Union 1996. May be photocopied by the church or organisation that has bought this book.

Always include food in sessions – where people bring and share a meal – and activities that involve interaction, for example personal story telling, games, including board games, kite-making, singing, a scavenger hunt, Bible study which needs to be done creatively, not just a question-and-answer session. Through the processes of being together, people's lives will be enriched. They will learn more about themselves, their worth, values and beliefs, and about others who may think and believe differently.

WARNING

A household cluster can help individuals and households in their 'scrap happy journey' of life. Through *Scrap Happy* we have seen that life is messy, and it will be so in a household cluster. We hope that a cluster will provide an arena for valuing difference, exercising patience, tolerance, kindness and forgiveness. In other words, people are given the opportunity to practice the skills necessary for living more christianly together. This requires sensitive leadership by those able to work intergenerationally.

THE CHURCHES

Churches are often well placed to organise household clusters as one aspect of their family ministry. Enabling friendships to be built and support to be on hand is a form of pastoral care that helps to strengthen home life. Many such groups become places for spiritual growth – as people share life, they communicate their values and beliefs. Household clusters with church people in them may develop prayer support for each other and explore faith issues, as well as engage in creative Bible exploration. Doing these things with all ages together creates an enriching dynamic which is different from that created by peer groups.

Some churches might start by opening their house groups to the children of members on a regular basis. Churches wanting to support people in the wider community as well as their own households may well develop clusters that enable friendships to be built between church and non-church households. People who live in the same street could develop their neighbourliness – often a simple structure like a cluster will give people permission to drop the British reserve and exercise the goodwill that is within them.

For further information and help with setting up and leading household clusters, contact the Family Ministry Consultant, Scripture Union Training Unit, 26–30 Heathcoat Street, Nottingham, NG1 3AA.

© Copyright Scripture Union 1996. May be photocopied by the church or organisation that has bought this book.

SCRAP HAPPY

Words and music: Philip Hawthorn

Chorus:
Scrap happy, Scrap happy!
Everybody is somebody.
Scrap happy, Scrap happy!
If you don't believe me
Just remember we are members of the
Big scrap happy family.
Just remember we are members of the
Big scrap happy family.

1. Take a pack of cards, and spend all day
   To build a tower this tall.
   Now take any one right away
   And the tower will fall.
   All the cards are needed as much as all the rest,
   And Jesus wants to be your friend,
   He says everybody is the best.

   Chorus

2. No one should ever be all alone,
   If we know how to care.
   No one should ever feel far from home
   When we've learnt how to share.
   Just as Jesus loves us all so faithfully
   He'll help us to love each other
   In the big Scrap Happy Family!

   Chorus

© 1989 Philip Hawthorn

SCRAP CAT CHORUS

Words and music: Philip Hawthorn

1. When the night is black,
   We all stretch our backs
   And call to all the maulers
   In their scrap cat sacks.
   Silently we slip
   To your window lip,
   And put a sudden finish
   To your kip.

   Chorus:
   Cause we're the scrap cat chorus!
   No, you can't ignore us!
   We're a streamline, feline company
   And we sing in *purr*-fect har-*meow*-ny.

2. Dinner time's a grin.
   We prowl around the bins
   And finish off a fish
   Inside a rusty tin.
   Then we feel all right.
   A juicy fish is quite
   The thing to make us sing
   A tune a night.

   Chorus

3. Fleas are in your fur,
   Friends, they say 'Oo-er'.
   Here's the place to make your face
   A great big purr.
   Happy in the scrap,
   Milk of love on tap,
   There'll always be a warm
   And comfy lap (me-ow)!

   Chorus

4. Cats on a caterwaul,
   Our claws they cause a call.
   Mercilessly cursing
   As we carefully crawl.
   Then home, our heads caress,
   Soft and smooth and, yes,
   Cursing kindly kittens,
   We're the best! (Oh yes!)

   Chorus (Repeat twice)

© 1989 Philip Hawthorn

DEM BONES

Traditional song   Words for verse 4: Philip Hawthorn

Chorus:
Dem bones, dem bones, dem dry bones,
Dem bones, dem bones, dem dry bones,
Dem bones, dem bones, dem dry bones,
Now hear the word of the Lord.

1. The head bone's connected to the neck bone,
   The neck bone's connected to the shoulder bone,
   The shoulder bone's connected to the back bone,
   Now hear the word of the Lord.

   Chorus

2. The back bone's connected to the hip bone,
   The hip bone's connected to the thigh bone,
   The thigh bone's connected to the knee bone,
   Now hear the word of the Lord.

   Chorus

3. The knee bone's connected to the leg bone,
   The leg bone's connected to the ankle bone,
   The ankle bone's connected to the foot bone,
   Now hear the word of the Lord.

   Chorus

4. Now we all need each other,
   Grandparents, sisters and brothers,
   Our friends and fathers and mothers,
   Now hear the word of the Lord.

   Chorus

Verse 4 © 1989 Philip Hawthorn

Piecing it together

Word Search Answers from page 66.

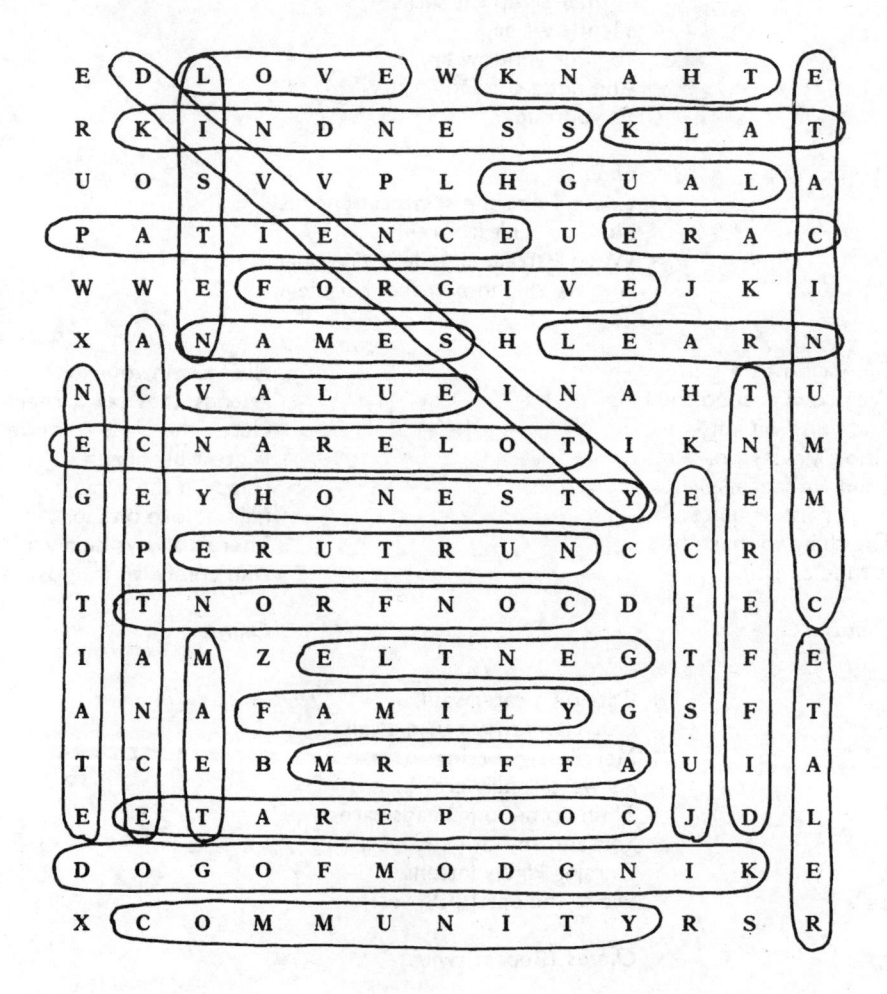

```
E D L O V E W K N A H T E
R K I N D N E S S K L A T
U O S V V P L H G U A L A
P A T I E N C E U E R A C
W W E F O R G I V E J K I
X A N A M E S H L E A R N
N C V A L U E I N A H T U
E C N A R E L O T I K N M
G E Y H O N E S T Y E E M
O P E R U T R U N C C R O
T T N O R F N O C D I E C
I A M Z E L T N E G T F E
A N A F A M I L Y G S F T
T C E B M R I F F A U I A
E E T A R E P O O C J D L
  D O G O F M O D G N I K E
X C O M M U N I T Y R S R
```

© Copyright Scripture Union 1996. May be photocopied by the church or organisation that has bought this book.